Exploring SE for Android

Discover Security Enhancements (SE) for Android
to build your own protected Android-based systems

William Confer

William Roberts

BIRMINGHAM - MUMBAI

Exploring SE for Android

First published: February 2015

Production reference: 1190215

Published by Packt Publishing Ltd.
Livery Place
35 Livery Street
Birmingham B3 2PB, UK.

ISBN 978-1-78439-059-4

www.packtpub.com

Credits

Foreword

The first talk of SELinux on Android started almost as soon as Android was announced. The interest at that time was mainly shown by academic circles and developers of SELinux itself. As a longtime user of SELinux in server deployments, I knew its benefits from a security point of view and also knew how much Android could benefit from them.

At that time, I may have been coy about the reasons I wanted to commit some of the initial patches to the SELinux project. Looking back at the code reviews for those Android Open Source Project (AOSP) changes, I now remember how much resistance there was in the beginning. Space on devices was at a premium, and it was considered a victory if we could save a few kilobytes. And here were the SELinux libraries and policies that increased the system size by thirty kilobytes! The performance impact had not even been measured at that time.

The work continued unabated with SELinux contributors, such as Stephen Smalley, Robert Craig, Joshua Brindle, and an author of this book, William Roberts, as well as with the help of my coworkers Geremy Condra and Nick Kralevich at Google. Slowly, through the herculean efforts of everyone involved, the project materialized and became more and more complete. Since Android 4.4 KitKat, SELinux is shipped in enforcing mode, and all Android users can benefit from the added protection that it affords.

The tale doesn't end there! Now, it's your turn to learn. This book is the first reference available for the specific flavor of SELinux found in Android. It's my sincere hope that this book imparts the knowledge you need to understand and contribute to its continued development. William Roberts has been submitting code to AOSP since the beginning of SELinux for Android, and his and Dr. Confer's knowledge is contained in these pages. It's up to you to read it and help write the next chapter of this saga.

Kenny Root

Mountain View, CA

About the Authors

William Confer has been engineering embedded and mobile systems since 1997. He has worked for Samsung Mobile as a managing staff engineer and currently teaches computer science at SUNY Polytechnic Institute. He holds a patent in low-cost character recognition for extremely resource-limited devices and has multiple other patents pending for mobile technologies.

> My wife, Ása, sacrificed endlessly to help give me the space and time needed for this work, and I owe her more than I can say. My three daughters also ensured I couldn't always be working on this book and distracted me in the best possible ways. I couldn't rest if I didn't thank all my fall 2014 students from SUNY Polytechnic Institute who put up with me when I was sidetracked by this book. Finally, and most importantly, my greatest thanks goes to my coauthor (and friend, student, and teacher), William Roberts, without whom I would have to have found another.

William Roberts is a software engineer who is focused on OS-level security and platform enhancements. He is one of the engineers who founded the Samsung KNOX product and an early adopter of SE for Android. He has made contributions to several open source projects, such as SE for Android, the Android Open Source Project, the Linux Kernel, CyanogenMod, and OpenSC. His recent interests have taken him to Smart Card technologies and the virtualization of smart cards. In his spare time, he works with Dr. Confer on the Miniat project (`http://www.miniat.org`), a virtual, embedded architecture simulator.

I would like to thank Dr. William Confer, the coauthor, for helping me write this book; his contributions were invaluable. Also, I would like to thank my wife for supporting me and giving me the time to do this, even though we were renovating the house. Also, I would like to thank my family and friends for their encouragement along the way.

About the Reviewers

Joshua Brindle is the CTO and cofounder of Quark Security Inc., a company focused on solving mobile and cross-domain security problems. Joshua has 12 years of professional experience in the area of development for government, academic, and open source software that focuses on security in Linux. Joshua has contributed to numerous open source projects, both as a project maintainer and as a developer. His work can be found on all SELinux systems and nearly all Linux systems. Joshua's recent experience focuses on building secure mobile devices using technologies such as Security Enhancements for Android, mobile device, and application management.

Hiromu Yakura is a student at Nada High School, Japan. He is the youngest person to hold the national information security qualification from Japan. He has given lectures about SE for Android at many conferences. He is also familiar with the security competition, Capture the Flag (CTF), and has participated in DEF CON CTF 2014 as a team binja.

I would like to express my gratitude to my family for their understanding and support.

www.PacktPub.com

Support files, eBooks, discount offers, and more

For support files and downloads related to your book, please visit www.PacktPub.com.

Did you know that Packt offers eBook versions of every book published, with PDF and ePub files available? You can upgrade to the eBook version at www.PacktPub.com and as a print book customer, you are entitled to a discount on the eBook copy. Get in touch with us at service@packtpub.com for more details.

At www.PacktPub.com, you can also read a collection of free technical articles, sign up for a range of free newsletters and receive exclusive discounts and offers on Packt books and eBooks.

https://www2.packtpub.com/books/subscription/packtlib

Do you need instant solutions to your IT questions? PacktLib is Packt's online digital book library. Here, you can search, access, and read Packt's entire library of books.

Why subscribe?

- Fully searchable across every book published by Packt
- Copy and paste, print, and bookmark content
- On demand and accessible via a web browser

Free access for Packt account holders

If you have an account with Packt at www.PacktPub.com, you can use this to access PacktLib today and view 9 entirely free books. Simply use your login credentials for immediate access.

Table of Contents

Preface   **1**

Chapter 1: Linux Access Controls   **7**

Changing permission bits   **10**

Changing owners and groups   **14**

The case for more   **15**

Capabilities model   **16**

Android's use of DAC   **17**

Glancing at Android vulnerabilities   **17**

Skype vulnerability   18

GingerBreak   18

Rage against the cage   18

MotoChopper   19

Summary   **19**

Chapter 2: Mandatory Access Controls and SELinux   **21**

Getting back to the basics   **22**

Labels   **23**

Users   23

Roles   23

Types   23

Access vectors   **24**

Multilevel security   **24**

Putting it together   **25**

Complexities and best practices   **30**

Summary   **30**

Chapter 3: Android Is Weird — 31

Android's security model — 31
Binder — 33
    Binder's architecture — 34
    Binder and security — 36
Zygote – application spawn — 37
The property service — 38
Summary — 39

Chapter 4: Installation on the UDOO — 41

Retrieving the source — 42
Flashing image on an SD card — 45
UDOO serial and Android Debug Bridge — 46
Flipping the switch — 49
It's alive — 53
Summary — 54

Chapter 5: Booting the System — 55

Policy load — 56
Fixing the policy version — 60
Summary — 62

Chapter 6: Exploring SELinuxFS — 63

Locating the filesystem — 63
Interrogating the filesystem — 64
    The enforce node — 65
    The disable file interface — 66
    The policy file — 66
    The null file — 67
    The mls file — 67
    The status file — 67
    Access Vector Cache — 68
    The booleans directory — 69
    The class directory — 70
    The initial_contexts directory — 71
    The policy_capabilities directory — 72
    ProcFS — 72
Java SELinux API — 73
Summary — 74

Chapter 7: Utilizing Audit Logs — 75

Upgrades – patches galore — 76
The audit system — 79
  The auditd daemon — 80
  Auditd internals — 81
Interpreting SELinux denial logs — 83
Contexts — 85
Summary — 88

Chapter 8: Applying Contexts to Files — 89

Labeling filesystems — 89
  fs_use — 90
  fs_task_use — 90
  fs_use_trans — 91
  genfscon — 91
  Mount options — 92
  Labeling with extended attributes — 92
  The file_contexts file — 93
  Dynamic type transitions — 95
Examples and tools — 96
  Fixing up /data — 103
A side note on security — 104
Summary — 104

Chapter 9: Adding Services to Domains — 105

Init – the king of daemons — 105
Dynamic domain transitions — 111
Explicit contexts via seclabel — 113
Relabeling processes — 114
Limitations on app labeling — 118
Summary — 118

Chapter 9: Placing Applications in Domains — 119

The case to secure the zygote — 119
Fortifying the zygote — 120
  Plumbing the zygote socket — 121
  The mac_permissions.xml file — 126
  keys.conf — 129
  seapp_contexts — 130
Summary — 138

Chapter 10: Labeling Properties   139
Labeling via property_contexts   139
Permissions on properties   140
Relabeling existing properties   141
Creating and labeling new properties   143
Special properties   144
   Control properties   144
   Persistent properties   144
   SELinux properties   145
Summary   145

Chapter 11: Mastering the Tool Chain   147
Building subcomponents – targets and projects   147
Exploring sepolicy's Android.mk   149
   Building sepolicy   150
   Controlling the policy build   152
   Digging deeper into build_policy   155
   Building mac_permissions.xml   157
   Building seapp_contexts   158
   Building file_contexts   158
   Building property_contexts   158
   Current NSA research files   158
Standalone tools   159
   sepolicy-check   159
   sepolicy-analyze   159
Summary   160

Chapter 12: Getting to Enforcing Mode   161
Updating to SEPolicy master   161
Purging the device   162
Setting up CTS   163
Running CTS   163
Gathering the results   164
   CTS test results   164
   Audit logs   165
Authoring device policy   165
   adbd   165
   bootanim   169
   debuggerd   170
   drmserver   170

dumpstate	171
installd	171
keystore	171
mediaserver	172
netd	172
rild	173
servicemanager	173
surfaceflinger	173
system_server	173
toolbox	174
untrusted_app	175
vold	176
watchdogd	176
wpa	177
Second policy pass	**178**
init	178
shell	180
init_shell.te	180
Field trials	**181**
Going enforcing	**181**
Summary	**182**
Appendix: The Development Environment	**183**
VirtualBox	**184**
Ubuntu Linux 12.04 (precise pangolin)	**184**
VirtualBox extension pack and guest additions	**186**
VirtualBox extension pack	186
VirtualBox guest additions	187
Save time with shared folders	**187**
The build environment	**188**
Oracle Java 6	**188**
Summary	**189**
Index	**191**

Preface

This book introduces the Security Enhancements (SE) for Android open source project and walks you through the process of securing new embedded systems with SE for Android. To our knowledge, this book is the first source to document such a process in its entirety so that students, DIY hobbyists, and engineers can create custom systems secured by SE for Android. Generally, only original equipment manufacturers (OEMs) do this, and quite commonly, the target device is a phone or tablet. We truly hope our book will change that, engaging a wide audience in development so they can use and understand these modern security tools.

We worked very hard to ensure this text is not just a step-by-step technology book. Specifically, we've chosen a model that directs you to fail your way to success. You will first gain appropriate theoretical understanding of how security is gained and enforced. Then we will introduce a system that has never been secured that way (not even by us, prior to writing this book). Next, we'll guide you through all our intelligent guesswork, embracing unexpected failures for the newly found idiosyncrasies they expose, and eventually enforcing our custom security policies. It requires you to learn to resolve differences between major open source projects such as SELinux, SE for Android, and Google Android, each of which has independent goals and deployment schedules. This prepares you to secure other devices, the process for which is always different, but hopefully, will now be more accessible.

What this book covers

Chapter 1, *Linux Access Controls*, discusses the basics of Discretionary Access Control (DAC), how some Android exploits leverage DAC problems, and demonstrate the need for more robust solutions.

Chapter 2, *Mandatory Access Controls and SELinux*, examines Mandatory Access Control (MAC) and its manifestation in SELinux. This chapter also explores tangible policy to control SELinux object interaction.

Chapter 3, Android Is Weird, introduces the Android security model and investigates binder, zygote, and the property service.

Chapter 4, Installation on the UDOO, walks through building and deploying Android from source to the UDOO-embedded board and turns on SELinux support.

Chapter 5, Booting the System, follows the boot process from the policy loading perspective and corrects issues to get SELinux to a usable state on the UDOO.

Chapter 6, Exploring SELinuxFS, examines the SELinuxFS filesystem and how it provides the kernel-to-userspace interface for higher-level idioms.

Chapter 7, Utilizing Audit Logs, investigates the audit subsystem, revealing how to interpret SELinux audit logs for the benefit of policy writing.

Chapter 8, Applying Contexts to Files, teaches you how filesystems and filesystem objects get their labels and contexts, demonstrating techniques to change them, including dynamic type transitions.

Chapter 9, Adding Services to Domains, emphasizes process labeling, notably the Android services run and managed by init.

Chapter 10, Placing Applications in Domains, shows you how to properly label the private data directories of applications, as well as application runtime contexts via configuration files and SELinux policy.

Chapter 11, Labeling Properties, demonstrates how to create and label new and existing properties, and some of the anomalies that occur when doing so.

Chapter 12, Mastering the Tool Chain, covers how the various components that control policy on the device are actually built and created. This chapter reviews the Android.mk components, detailing how the heart of the build and configuration management works.

Chapter 13, Getting to Enforcing Mode, utilizes all the skills you learned in the earlier chapters to respond to audit logs from CTS and get the UDOO in enforcing mode.

Appendix, The Development Environment, walks you through the necessary steps of setting up a Linux environment suitable for you to follow all the activities in this book.

What you need for this book

Hardware requirements include:

- A UDOO-embedded development board
- An 8 GB Mini SD card (while you can use a card with greater capacity, we do not recommended it)
- A minimum of 16GB of RAM
- At least 80 GB of free hard drive space

Software requirements include:

- An Ubuntu 12.04 LTS desktop system
- Oracle JDK 6.0 version 6u45
- Some additional miscellaneous Linux software is required, but these are described in the book and are available for free.

Who this book is for

This book is intended for developers and engineers who are somewhat familiar with operating system concepts as implemented by Linux. They could be hobbyists wanting to secure their Android-powered creations, OEM engineers building handsets, or engineers from emerging areas where Android is seeing growth. A basic background in C programming will be helpful.

Conventions

In this book, you will find a number of text styles that distinguish between different kinds of information. Here are some examples of these styles and explanations of their meanings.

Code words in text, database table names, folder names, filenames, file extensions, pathnames, dummy URLs, user input, and Twitter handles are shown as follows: "Now let's attempt to execute the `hello.txt` file and see what happens."

A block of code is set as follows:

```
case INTERFACE_TRANSACTION:
{
reply.writeString(DESCRIPTOR);
return true;
}
```

Any command-line input or output is written as follows:

$ su testuser

Password:

testuser@ubuntu:/home/bookuser$

New terms and **important words** are shown in bold. Words that you see on the screen, for example, in menus or dialog boxes, appear in the text like this: "Exit the configuration menus by selecting **Exit** until you are asked to save your new configuration."

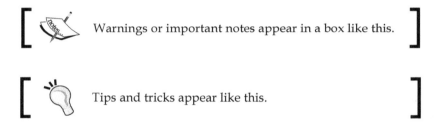

Warnings or important notes appear in a box like this.

Tips and tricks appear like this.

Reader feedback

Feedback from our readers is always welcome. Let us know what you think about this book—what you liked or disliked. Reader feedback is important for us as it helps us develop titles that you will really get the most out of.

To send us general feedback, simply e-mail feedback@packtpub.com, and mention the book's title in the subject of your message.

If there is a topic that you have expertise in and you are interested in either writing or contributing to a book, see our author guide at www.packtpub.com/authors.

Customer support

Now that you are the proud owner of a Packt book, we have a number of things to help you to get the most from your purchase.

Downloading the example code

You can download the example code files from your account at http://www.packtpub.com for all the Packt Publishing books you have purchased. If you purchased this book elsewhere, you can visit http://www.packtpub.com/support and register to have the files e-mailed directly to you.

Errata

Although we have taken every care to ensure the accuracy of our content, mistakes do happen. If you find a mistake in one of our books—maybe a mistake in the text or the code—we would be grateful if you could report this to us. By doing so, you can save other readers from frustration and help us improve subsequent versions of this book. If you find any errata, please report them by visiting http://www.packtpub.com/submit-errata, selecting your book, clicking on the **Errata Submission Form** link, and entering the details of your errata. Once your errata are verified, your submission will be accepted and the errata will be uploaded to our website or added to any list of existing errata under the Errata section of that title.

To view the previously submitted errata, go to https://www.packtpub.com/books/content/support and enter the name of the book in the search field. The required information will appear under the **Errata** section.

Piracy

Piracy of copyrighted material on the Internet is an ongoing problem across all media. At Packt, we take the protection of our copyright and licenses very seriously. If you come across any illegal copies of our works in any form on the Internet, please provide us with the location address or website name immediately so that we can pursue a remedy.

Please contact us at copyright@packtpub.com with a link to the suspected pirated material.

We appreciate your help in protecting our authors and our ability to bring you valuable content.

Questions

If you have a problem with any aspect of this book, you can contact us at questions@packtpub.com, and we will do our best to address the problem.

1
Linux Access Controls

Android is an operating system composed of two distinct components. The first component is a forked mainline Linux kernel and shares almost everything in common with Linux. The second component, which will be discussed later, is the user space portion, which is very custom and Android specific. Since the Linux kernel underpins this system and is responsible for the majority of access control decisions, it is the logical place to begin a detailed look at Android.

In this chapter we will:

- Examine the basics of Discretionary Access Control
- Introduce Linux permissions flags and capabilities
- Trace syscalls as we validate access policies
- Make the case for more robust access control technology
- Discuss Android exploits that leverage problems with Discretionary Access Control

Linux's default and familiar access control mechanism is called **Discretionary Access Control (DAC)**. This is just a term that means permissions regarding access to an object are at the discretion of its creator/owner.

In Linux, when a process invokes most system calls, a permission check is performed. As an example, a process wishing to open a file would invoke the open() syscall. When this syscall is invoked, a context switch is performed, and the operating system code is executed. The OS has the ability to determine whether a file descriptor should be returned to the requesting process or not. During this decision-making process, the OS checks the access permissions of both the requesting process and the target file it wishes to obtain the file descriptor to. Either the file descriptor or EPERM is returned, dependent on whether the permission checks pass or fail respectively.

Linux maintains data structures in the kernel for managing these permission fields, which are accessible from user space, and ones that should be familiar to Linux and *NIX users alike. The first set of access control metadata belongs to the process, and forms a portion of its credential set. The common credentials are user and group. In general, we use the term group to mean both primary group and possible secondary group(s). You can view these permissions by running the ps command:

```
$ ps -eo pid,comm,user,group,supgrp
PID COMMAND            USER      GROUP      SUPGRP
1 init                root      root       -
...
 2993 system-service- root      root       root
 3276 chromium-browse bookuser sudo fuse bookuser
...
```

As you can see, we have processes running as the users root and bookuser. You can also see that their primary group is only one part of the equation. Processes also have a secondary set of groups called supplementary groups. This set might be empty, indicated by the dash in the SUPGRP field.

The file we wish to open, referred to as the target object, target, or object also maintains a set of permissions. The object maintains USER and GROUP, as well as a set of permission bits. In the context of the target object, USER can be referred to as *owner* or *creator*.

```
$ ls -la
total 296
drwxr-xr-x 38 bookuser bookuser  4096 Aug 23 11:08 .
drwxr-xr-x  3 root     root      4096 Jun  8 18:50 ..
-rw-rw-r--  1 bookuser bookuser   116 Jul 22 13:13 a.c
drwxrwxr-x  4 bookuser bookuser  4096 Aug  4 16:20 .android
-rw-rw-r--  1 bookuser bookuser   130 Jun 19 17:51 .apport-ignore.xml
```

```
-rw-rw-r--  1 bookuser bookuser   365 Jun 23 19:44 hello.txt
-rw-------  1 bookuser bookuser 19276 Aug  4 16:36 .bash_history
...
```

If we look at the preceding command's output, we can see that hello.txt has a USER of bookuser and GROUP as bookuser. We can also see the permission bits or flags on the left-hand side of the output. There are seven fields to consider as well. Each empty field is denoted with a dash. When printed with ls, the first fields can get convoluted by semantics. For this reason, let's use stat to investigate the file permissions:

```
$ stat hello.txt
  File: `hello.txt'
  Size: 365          Blocks: 8          IO Block: 4096    regular file
Device: 801h/2049d  Inode: 1587858      Links: 1
Access: (0664/-rw-rw-r--)  Uid: ( 1000/bookuser)    Gid: ( 1000/bookuser)
Access: 2014-08-04 15:53:01.951024557 -0700
Modify: 2014-06-23 19:44:14.308741592 -0700
Change: 2014-06-23 19:44:14.308741592 -0700
 Birth: -
```

The first access line is the most compelling. It contains all the important information for the access controls. The second line is just a timestamp letting us know when the file was last accessed. As we can see, USER or UID of the object is bookuser, and GROUP is bookuser as well. The permission flags, (0664/-rw-rw-r--), identify the two ways that permission flags are represented. The first, the octal form 0664, condenses each three-flag field into one of the three base-8 (octal) digits. The second is the friendly form, -rw-rw-r--, equivalent to the octal form but easier to interpret visually. In either case, we can see the leftmost field is 0, and the rest of our discussions will ignore it. That field is for setuid and setgid capabilities, which is not important for this discussion. If we convert the remaining octal digits, 664, to binary, we get 110 110 100. This binary representation directly relates to the friendly form. Each triple maps to read, write, and execute permissions. Often you will see this permission triple represented as RWX. The first triple are the permissions given to USER, the second are the permissions given to GROUP, and the third is what is given to OTHERS. Translating to conventional English would yield, "The user, bookuser, has permission to read from and write to hello.txt. The group, bookuser, has permission to read from and write to hello.txt, and everyone else has permission only to read from hello.txt." Let's test this with some real-world examples.

Changing permission bits

Let's test the access controls in the example running processes as user `bookuser`.
Most processes run in the context of the user that invoked them (excluding `setuid`
and `getuid` programs), so any command we invoke should inherit our user's
permissions. We can view it by issuing:

```
$ groups bookuser
bookuser : bookuser sudo fuse
```

My user, `bookuser`, is `USER bookuser`, `GROUP bookuser` and `SUPGRP sudo`
and `fuse`.

To test for read access, we can use the `cat` command, which opens the file and prints
its content to `stdout`:

```
$ cat hello.txt
Hello, "Exploring SE for Android"
Here is a simple text file for
your enjoyment.
...
```

We can introspect the syscalls executed by running the `strace` command and
viewing the output:

```
$ strace cat hello.txt
...
open("hello.txt", O_RDONLY)                = 3
...
read(3, "Hello, \"Exploring SE for Android\"\n"..., 32768) = 365
...
```

The output can be quite verbose, so I am only showing the relevant parts. We can see
that `cat` invoked the `open` syscall and obtained the file descriptor 3. We can use that
descriptor to find other accesses via other syscalls. Later we will see a read occurring
on file descriptor 3, which returns 365, the number of bytes read. If we didn't have
permission to read from `hello.txt`, the open would fail, and we would never have
a valid file descriptor for the file. We would additionally see the failure in the `strace`
output.

Now that read permission is verified, let's try write. One simple way to do this is to
write a simple program that writes something to the existing file. In this case, we will
write the line `my new text\n` (refer to `write.c`.)

Compile the program using the following command:

```
$ gcc -o mywrite write.c
```

Now run using the newly compiled program:

```
$ strace ./mywrite hello.txt
```

On verification, you will see:

```
...
open("hello.txt", O_WRONLY)              = 3
write(3, "my new text\n", 12)       = 12
...
```

As you can see, the write succeeded and returned 12, the number of bytes written to hello.txt. No errors were reported, so the permissions seem in check so far.

Now let's attempt to execute hello.txt and see what happens. We are expecting to see an error. Let's execute it like a normal command:

```
$ ./hello.txt
bash: ./hello.txt: Permission denied
```

This is exactly what we expected, but let's invoke it with strace to gain a deeper understanding of what failed:

```
$ strace ./hello.txt
...
execve("./hello.txt", ["./hello.txt"], [/* 39 vars */]) = -1 EACCES
(Permission denied)
...
```

The execve system call, which launches processes, failed with EACCESS. This is just the sort of thing one would hope for when no execute permission is given. The Linux access controls worked as expected!

Let's test the access controls in the context of another user. First, we'll create a new user called testuser using the adduser command:

```
$ sudo adduser testuser
[sudo] password for bookuser:
Adding user `testuser' ...
Adding new group `testuser' (1001) ...
Adding new user `testuser' (1001) with group `testuser' ...
```

```
Creating home directory `/home/testuser' ...
```

`...`

Verify the USER, GROUP, and SUPGRP of `testuser`:

```
$ groups testuser
testuser : testuser
```

Since the USER and GROUP do not match any of the permissions on `a.s`, all accesses will be subject to the OTHERS permissions checks, which if you recall, is read only (`0664`).

Start by temporarily working as `testuser`:

```
$ su testuser
Password:
testuser@ubuntu:/home/bookuser$
```

As you can see, we are still in bookuser's home directory, but the current user has been changed to `testuser`.

We will start by testing `read` with the `cat` command:

```
$ strace cat hello.txt
...
open("hello.txt", O_RDONLY)             = 3
...
read(3, "my new text\n", 32768)     = 12
...
```

Similar to the earlier example, `testuser` can read the data just fine, as expected.

Now let's move on to write. The expectation is that this will fail without appropriate access:

```
$ strace ./mywrite hello.txt
...
open("hello.txt", O_WRONLY)             = -1 EACCES (Permission
denied)
...
```

As expected, the syscall operation failed. When we attempt to execute `hello.txt` as `testuser`, this should fail as well:

```
$ strace ./hello.txt
...
```

```
execve("./hello.txt", ["./hello.txt"], [/* 40 vars */]) = -1 EACCES
(Permission denied)
...
```

Now we need to test the group access permissions. We can do this by adding a supplementary group to testuser. To do this, we need to exit to bookuser, who has permissions to execute the sudo command:

```
$ exit
exit
$ sudo usermod -G bookuser testuser
```

Now let's check the groups of testuser:

```
$ groups testuser
testuser : testuser bookuser
```

As a result of the previous usermod command testuser now belongs to two groups: testuser and bookuser. That means when testuser accesses a file or other object (such as a socket) with the group bookuser, the GROUP permissions, rather than OTHERS, will apply to it. In the context of hello.txt, testuser can now read from and write to the file, but not execute it.

Switch to testuser by executing the following command:

```
$ su testuser
```

Test read by executing the following command:

```
$ strace cat ./hello.txt
...
open("./hello.txt", O_RDONLY)               = 3
...
read(3, "my new text\n", 32768)      = 12
...
```

As before, testuser is able to read the file. The only difference is that it can now read the file through the access permissions of OTHERS and GROUP.

Test write by executing the following command:

```
$ strace ./mywrite hello.txt
...
open("hello.txt", O_WRONLY)                  = 3
write(3, "my new text\n", 12)        = 12
...
```

This time, `testuser` was able to write the file as well, instead of failing with the `EACCESS` permission error shown before.

Attempting to execute the file should still fail:

```
$ strace ./hello.txt
execve("./hello.txt", ["./hello.txt"], [/* 40 vars */]) = -1 EACCES
(Permission denied)
...
```

These concepts are the foundation of Linux access control permission bits, users and groups.

Changing owners and groups

Using `hello.txt` for exploratory work in the previous sections, we have shown how the owner of an object can allow various forms of access by managing the permission bits of the object. Changing the permissions is accomplished using the `chmod` syscall. Changing the user and/or group is done with the `chown` syscall. In this section, we will investigate the details of these operations in action.

Let's start by granting read and write permissions only to the owner of `hello.txt` file, `bookuser`.

```
$ chmod 0600 hello.txt
$ stat hello.txt
  File: `hello.txt'
  Size: 12          Blocks: 8          IO Block: 4096    regular file
Device: 801h/2049d  Inode: 1587858     Links: 1
Access: (0600/-rw-------)  Uid: ( 1000/bookuser)   Gid: ( 1000/bookuser)
Access: 2014-08-23 12:34:30.147146826 -0700
Modify: 2014-08-23 12:47:19.123113845 -0700
Change: 2014-08-23 12:59:04.275083602 -0700
 Birth: -
```

As we can see, the file permissions are now set to only allow read and write access for `bookuser`. A thorough reader could execute the commands from earlier sections in this chapter to verify that permissions work as expected.

Changing the group can be done in a similar fashion with `chown`. Let's change the group to `testuser`:

```
$ chown bookuser:testuser hello.txt
chown: changing ownership of `hello.txt': Operation not permitted
```

This did not work as we intended, but what is the issue? In Linux, only privileged processes can change the USER and GROUP fields of objects. The initial USER and GROUP fields are set during object creation from the effective USER and GROUP, which are checked when attempting to execute that process. Only processes create objects. Privileged processes come in two forms: those running as the almighty root and those that have their capabilities set. We will dive into the details of capabilities later. For now, let's focus on the root.

Let's change the user to root to ensure executing the chown command will change the group of that object:

```
$ sudo su
# chown bookuser:testuser hello.txt
Now, we can verify the change occurred successfully:
# stat hello.txt
  File: `hello.txt'
  Size: 12          Blocks: 8          IO Block: 4096    regular file
Device: 801h/2049d  Inode: 1587858     Links: 1
Access: (0600/-rw-------)  Uid: ( 1000/bookuser)   Gid: ( 1001/testuser)
Access: 2014-08-23 12:34:30.147146826 -0700
Modify: 2014-08-23 12:47:19.123113845 -0700
Change: 2014-08-23 13:08:46.059058649 -0700
 Birth: -
```

The case for more

You can see the GROUP (GID) is now testuser, and things seem reasonably secure because in order to change the user and group of an object, you need to be privileged. You can only change the permission bits on an object if you own it, with the exception of the root user. This means that if you're running as root, you can do whatever you like to the system, even without permission. This absolute authority is why a successful attack or an error on a root running process can cause grave damage to the system. Also, a successful attack on a non-root process could also cause damage by inadvertently changing the permissions bits. For example, suppose there is an unintended chmod 0666 command on your SSH private key. This would expose your secret key to all users on the system, which is almost certainly something you would never want to happen. The root limitation is partially addressed by the capabilities model.

Capabilities model

For many operations on Linux, the object permission model doesn't quite fit. For instance, changing UID and GID requires some magical USER known as root. Suppose you have a long running service that needs to utilize some of these capabilities. Perhaps this service listens to kernel events and creates the device nodes for you? Such a service exists, and it's called ueventd or user event daemon. This daemon traditionally runs as root, which means if it is compromised, it could potentially read your private keys from your home directory and send them back to the attacker. This might be an extraordinary example, but it's meant to showcase that running processes as root can be dangerous. Suppose you could start a service as the root user and have the process change its UID and GID to something not privileged, but retain some smaller set of privileged capabilities to do its job? This is exactly what the capabilities model in Linux is.

The capabilities model in Linux is an attempt to break down the set of permissions that root has into smaller subsets. This way, processes can be confined to the set of minimum privileges they need to perform their intended function. This is known as least privilege, a key ideology when securing systems that minimizes the amount of damage a successful attack can do. In some instances, it can even prevent a successful attack from occurring by blocking an otherwise open attack vector.

There are many capabilities. The man page for capabilities is the de facto documentation. Let's take a look at the CAP_SYS_BOOT capability:

```
$ man capabilities

...

CAP_SYS_BOOT

        Use reboot(2) and kexec_load(2).
```

This means a process running with this capability can reboot the system. However, that process can't arbitrarily change USERS and GROUP as it could if it was running as root or with CAP_DAC_READ_SEARCH. This limits what an attacker can do:

```
<FROM MAN PAGE>

CAP_DAC_READ_SEARCH

        Bypass file read permission checks and directory read and exe⬚
                cute permission checks.
```

Now suppose the case where our restart process runs with CAP_CHOWN. Let's say it uses this capability to ensure that when a restart request is received, it backs up a file from each user's home directory to a server before restarting. Let's say this file is ~/backup, the permissions are 0600, and USER and GROUP are the respective user of that home directory. In this case, we have minimized the permissions as best we can, but the process could still access the users SSH keys and upload those either by error or attack. Another approach to this would be to set the group to backup and run the process with GROUP backup. However, this has limitations. Suppose you want to share this file with another user. That user would require a supplementary group of backup, but now the user can read *all* of the backup files, not just the ones intended. An astute reader might think about the bind mounts, however the process doing the bind mounts and file permissions also runs with some capability, and thus suffers from this granularity problem as well.

The major issue, and the case for another access control system can be summarized by one word, *granularity*. The DAC model doesn't have the granularity required to safely handle complex access control models or to minimize the amount of damage a process can do. This is particularly important on Android, where the entire isolation system is dependent on this control, and a rogue root process can compromise the whole system.

Android's use of DAC

In the Android sandbox model, every application runs as its own UID. This means that each app can separate its stored data from one another. The user and group are set to the UID and GID of that application, so no app can access the private files of an application without the application explicitly performing chmod on its objects. Also, applications in Android cannot have capabilities, so we don't have to worry about capabilities such as CAP_SYS_PTRACE, which is the ability to debug another application. In Android, in a perfect world, only system components run with privileges, and applications don't accidentally chmod private files for all to read. This issue was not corrected by the current AOSP SELinux policy due to app compatibility, but could be closed with SELinux. The proper way to share data between applications on Android is via binder, and sharing file descriptors. For smaller amounts of data, the provider model suffices.

Glancing at Android vulnerabilities

With our newly found understanding of the DAC permission model and some of its limitations, let's look at some Android exploits against it. We will cover only a few exploits to understand how the DAC model failed.

Skype vulnerability

CVE-2011-1717 was released in 2011. In this exploit, the Skype application left a SQLite3 database world readable (something analogous to 0666 permissions). This database contained usernames and chat logs, and personal data such as name and e-mail. An application called Skypwned was able to demonstrate this capability. This is an example of how being able to change the permissions on your objects could be bad, especially when the case opens READ to OTHERS.

GingerBreak

CVE-2011-1823 showcases a root attack on Android. The volume management daemon (vold) on Android is responsible for the mounting and unmounting of the external SD card. The daemon listens for messages over a NETLINK socket. The daemon never checked where the messages were sourced from, and any application could open and create a NETLINK socket to send messages to vold. Once the attacker opened the NETLINK socket, they sent a very carefully crafted message to bypass a sanity check. The check tested a signed integer for a maximum bound, but never checked it for negativity. It was then used to index an array. This negative access would lead to memory corruption and, with a proper message, could result in the execution of arbitrary code. The GingerBreak implementation resulted in an arbitrary user gaining root privileges, a textbook privilege execution attack. Once rooted, the device's sandboxes were no longer valid.

Rage against the cage

CVE-2010-EASY is a setuid exhaustion via fork bomb attack. It successfully attacks the adb daemon on Android, which starts life as root and downgrades its permissions if root is not needed. This attack keeps adb as root and returns a root shell to the user. In Linux kernel 2.6, the setuid system call returns an error when the number of running processes RLIMIT_NPROC is met. The adb daemon code does not check the return of setuid, which leaves a small race window open for the attacker. The attacker needs to fork enough processes to reach RLIMIT_NPROC and then kill the daemon. The adb daemon downgrades to shell UID and the attacker runs the program as shell USER, thus the kill will work. At this point, the adb service is respawned, and if RLIMIT_ NPROC is maxed out, setuid will fail and adb will stay running as root. Then, running adb shell from a host returns a nice root shell to the user.

MotoChopper

CVE-2013-2596 is a vulnerability in the mmap functionality of a Qualcomm video driver. Access to the GPU is provided by apps to do advanced graphics rendering such as in the case of OpenGL calls. The vulnerability in mmap allows the attacker to mmap kernel address space, at which point the attacker is able to directly change their kernel credential structure. This exploit is an example where the DAC model was not at fault. In reality, outside of patching the code or removing direct graphics access, nothing but programming checks of the mmap bounds could have prevented this attack.

Summary

The DAC model is extremely powerful, but its lack of fine granularity and use of an extraordinarily powerful root user leaves something to be desired. With the increasing sensitivity of mobile handset use, the case to increase the security of the system is well-founded. Thankfully, Android is built on Linux and thus benefits from a large ecosystem of engineers and researchers. Since the Linux Kernel 2.6, a new access control model called **Mandatory Access Controls (MAC)** was added. This is a framework by which modules can be loaded into the kernel to provide a new form of access control model. The very first module was called SELinux. It is used by Red Hat and others to secure sensitive government systems. Thus, a solution was found to enable such access controls for Android.

2
Mandatory Access Controls and SELinux

In *Chapter 1, Linux Access Controls*, we introduced some of the shortcomings of a discretionary access control system. In these systems, the owner of an object has full control over its permissions flags and can demonstrate greater capabilities (for example, the ability to chown) when executing as root or with certain capabilities. In this chapter, we will:

- Examine the fundamentals of MAC
- Introduce some industry drivers for SELinux
- Discuss labels, users, roles, and types
- Explore the implementation of tangible policy to allow and constrain object interaction

Ideal MAC systems maintain the property of providing definitive access controls on kernel resources, such as files, irrespective of an object's owner. For instance, with a MAC system, the owner of an object might not have full control of its permissions. In Linux, the MAC framework works orthogonally to the current DAC controls. This means that the MAC controls do not interfere with the DAC controls. In other words, to avoid potential conflicts between the MAC and DAC systems, the kernel validates access using the DAC permissions before checking the MAC permissions. If the DAC permissions result in a permissions violation, then the MAC permissions are never checked. The kernel will validate access against the MAC permissions provider only when the DAC permissions pass. Failure at either level will result in a return of EACCESS. If the DAC and the MAC permissions pass, then the kernel resource (for example, a file descriptor) is sent back to user space.

In Linux, a framework called the **Linux Security Module (LSM)** framework was merged during the Linux 2.6.x series of kernels. This framework allows you to enable the mandatory access control systems in a build time selection by tethering the LSM hooks to the security provider. **Security Enhanced Linux (SELinux)** is the first consumer of this MAC security framework within the kernel and is an implementation of a mandatory access control system. SELinux ships in a wide variety of Linux systems, such as **Red Hat Enterprise Linux (RHEL)** and consequently Fedora. Recently, it has begun shipping with Android. The source code for SELinux can be found in the Linux source code tree under `kernel/security/selinux` for those wishing to review it.

Getting back to the basics

SELinux is a reimplementation of a design engineered by the U.S. government and The University of Utah known as the **FLUX Advanced Security Kernel (FLASK)**. The SELinux and FLASK architecture provide a central policy file utilized while determining the results of access control decisions. This central policy is in a whitelist form. This means that all access control rules must be defined explicitly by the policy file. This policy file is abstracted and served by a software component called a security server. When the Linux kernel needs to make an access control decision and SELinux is enabled, the kernel interacts with the security server by means of the LSM hooks.

In a running system, a process is the active entity that gets time on the CPU to perform tasks. The user merely invokes these processes to do the work on their behalf. This is an important concept. As we type this book, we trust that the word processors running on our machines with our credentials aren't opening our SSH keys and embedding them in the document metadata. Right now, the process is in control of the computing resources, not the user. The process is the running entity, it is the process that makes system calls to the kernel for resources, not the physical human being. With this in mind, the very first actor in this SELinux system is the process, typically referred to as the **subject**. It is the subject that accesses files. It is the subject that the security server will use to make access decisions on.

Consequently, the subject utilizes kernel resources. This kind of kernel resource is an example of a **target**. The subject performs actions on the target. Naturally, one should ask, "What actions does a subject perform?" These are known as access vectors and typically correlate to the name of the syscall performed. For example, the subject could perform an `open` on the target. It is important to note that targets could be processes as well. For instance, if the system call is `ptrace`, the subject could be something along the lines of a debugger, and the target would be the process you wish to debug. A subject is frequently a process, but a target could be a process, socket, file, or something else.

Labels

SELinux provides semantics for describing policies related to the targets and subjects using labels. Labels are the metadata associated with an object that maintains the subject's and target's access information. The data associated with this object is a string. Returning to the debugger example, the `gdb` process might have a subject label string of `debugger`, and the target might have a label of `debugee`. Then in the security policy, some semantic could be used to express that processes with the subject label `debugger` are allowed to debug applications with target label `debugee`.

Fortunately, and perhaps unfortunately, SELinux does not use such simple labels. In fact, the labels are made up of four colon-delimited fields: user, role, type, and level. This additional complexity affords very flexible control options.

Users

The very first field in a label identifies the user. The user field is used as part of the design for **user-based access controls** (**UBAC**). However, this is not typically associated with human users as it is with the concept of users in DAC. SELinux users typically define a group of traditional users. A common example is to identify all normal users as the SELinux user, `user_u`. Perhaps a separate user for system processes, such as `system_u`. By convention in the desktop SELinux community, user portions of the string are suffixed with a `_u`.

Roles

The second field in a label is role. The role is used as part of the design for **role-based access controls** (**RBAC**). Roles are used to provide additional granularity to the user. For instance, suppose we have the user field, `sysadm_u`, reserved for administrators. The administrator might be in separate tasks, and depending on the tasks, the role (and therefore, privileges) of users in `sysadm_u` may change. For example, when an administrator needs to mount and unmount file systems, the role field might change to `mount_admin_r`. When an administrator is setting the `iptables` rules, the role might change to `net_admin_r`. Roles allow the isolation of privileges within the scope of the tasks being performed.

Types

Type is the third field of the colon-delimited label. The type field is evaluated during the **type enforcement** (**TE**) portion of SELinux's access control model. TE is the major component that drives SELinux's security capabilities, and it is at this point where the policy starts to take effect.

SELinux is based on a whitelist system where everything is denied by default and requires explicit approval from the policy for an interaction to occur. This approval is initially determined from the policy via an allow rule that references both the subject's and target's type. SELinux types can also be assigned attributes. Attributes allow you to give numerous types a common set of rules. Attributes can help minimize the amount of types, and can be used in fashion similar to that of an inheritance model.

Access vectors

Data is accessed by processes via system calls and possible user defined access methods. The user defined access methods are usually controlled via a userspace object manager. These access paths, also known as vectors, make up a set of actions that can be applied to the object. For instance, if a process opens a file, writes some data into the file, and then reads it back, the access vectors exercised would be `open`, `read`, and `write`. If a process debugs another process, the access vector would be `ptrace`.

Multilevel security

SELinux also supports a **multilevel security** (**MLS**) model, which pays homage to the **Bell-LaPadula** (**BLP**) model, but alternate models could be used. The BLP model was created to formalize the Department of Defense's security policies. For example, a person with a secret clearance should not be able to read top-secret material. However, let's suppose this person has a brilliant idea that ultimately needs to be protected at the top-secret level; that data could then be "up-classified" to top-secret. This is referred to as "no read up or write down".

The SELinux implementation of this field has subfields. The first field is sensitivity, and will always be present. In the context of the previous example, pertinent sensitivities include secret and top secret. The second subfield is category, and might not be present. These fields also make sense in the context of government classification. The data itself might be compartmentalized, so while the sensitivity is the same, such as top secret, the data should only be disseminated to people within the same compartment or category. Sensitivities are defined in a hierarchical fashion via the dominance keyword. In a typical policy, s0 is the lowest sensitivity and sN where $n > 0$ is the highest. Thus, s1 has a greater sensitivity than s0. Categories are sets. The controls associated with the level, which is comprised of sensitivities and potentially categories, follow set theory concepts, such as dominance and equality. In MLS security, all interactions are allowed by default, unlike type enforcement. Both the sensitivity and the category can be ranged, and categories can be enumerated. Thus, a label might have some number of sensitivities and different number of categories.

Putting it together

SELinux labels are quite flexible and sometimes complex. It's often beneficial to start with a contrived example that focuses on type enforcement. Later, we can add additional fields later as the need for finer granularity becomes more apparent. Conveniently, you can project this model to scenarios in everyday life to provide some sense of tangibility to the material. Dan Walsh, a prominent SELinux figure, posted a blog post using pets as an analogy. Let's continue on with that premise, but we will make some modifications as we go and define our own examples. It's best to start with simple type enforcement as it is the easiest to understand.

 You can read Dan Walsh's original blog post introducing the pet analogy at http://opensource.com/business/13/11/ selinux-policy-guide.

Suppose we own a cat and a dog. We don't want the cat to eat dog food. We don't want the dog to eat cat food. At this point, we have already identified two subjects, a cat and a dog, and two targets, cat food and dog food. We also have identified an access vector, eating. We can use allow rules to implement our policy. Possible rules could look like this:

```
allow cat cat_chow:food eat;
allow dog dog_chow:food eat;
```

Let's use this example to start and define a basic syntax for expressing the access controls we would like to enforce. The first token is allow, stating we wish to allow an interaction between a subject and a target. The dog is assigned the type, dog, and the cat, cat. The cat food is assigned the type cat_chow, and the dog food, dog_chow. The access vector in this case is eat. With this basic syntax, which is also valid SELinux syntax, we restrict the animals to the food they should eat. Notice the :food annotation after the type. This is the class field of the target object. For instance, there might also be dog_chow treat and cat_chow classes that could indicate our desire to allow access to treats in a fashion that is potentially different from the way we allow access to foods that are not treats.

Let's say we get two more dogs, and our scenario has three dogs. The dogs are of different sizes: small, medium, and large. We want to make sure none of these new dogs eat others' food. We could do something like create a new type for each of the dogs and prevent dogs from eating the food of other dogs. It would look something like this:

```
allow cat cat_chow:food eat;
allow dog_small dog_small_chow:food eat;
```

```
allow dog_medium dog_medium_chow:food eat;
allow dog_large dog_large chow:food eat;
```

This would work; however, the total number of types would be difficult to manage, and that would continue to grow if we allow the large dog to eat the smaller breeds' food. What we could do is use MLS support to assign a sensitivity to each target or dog food bowl. Let's assume the following:

- The cat's food bowl has sensitivity, `tiny`
- The small dog's food bowl has sensitivity, `small`
- The medium-sized dog's food bowl has sensitivity, `medium`
- The large dog's food bowl has sensitivity, `large`

We also need to make sure that the subjects are labeled with the proper sensitivity as well:

- The cat should have sensitivity, `tiny`
- The small dog should have sensitivity, `small`
- The medium-sized dog should have sensitivity, `medium`
- The large dog should have sensitivity, `large`

At this point, we need to introduce additional syntax to allow the interactions, since by default, MLS allows everything and TE denies everything. We'll use `mlsconstrain`, to restrict interactions within the system. The rule could look like this:

```
mlsconstrain food eat (l1 eq l2);
```

This constraint only allows subjects to eat food with the same sensitivity level. SELinux defines the keywords `l1` and `l2`. The `l1` keyword is the level of the target and `l2` is the level of the source. Because the rules are part of a whitelist, this also prevents subjects from eating food that does not have the equivalent sensitivity level.

Now, let's say we get yet another large dog. Now we have two large breed dogs. However, they have different diets and need to access different foods. We could add a new type or modify an existing type, but this would have the same limitations that led us to use sensitivities to prevent access. We could add another sensitivity, but it might get confusing that there are `large1` and `large2` sensitivities. At this point, categories would allow us to get a bit more granular in our controls. Suppose we add a category denoting the breed. Our MLS portion of our label would look something like this:

```
large:golden_retriever
large:black_lab
```

These could be used to prevent the black lab from eating the golden retriever's food. Now suppose you're surprised with another dog, a Saint Bernard. Let's say this new Bernard can eat any large dog's food, but the other large dogs can't eat his food. We could label the food bowls and the dogs.

Dog Breed	Subject label	Target label
Golden Retriever	`Dog:large:golden_retriver`	`dog_chow:large:golden_retriver`
Black Lab	`Dog:large:black_lab`	`dog_chow:large:black_lab`
Saint Bernard	`Dog:large:saint_bernard, black_lab, golden_retriever`	`dog_chow:large:saint_bernard`
Cat	`Cat:tiny`	`cat_chow:tiny`

The existing `mlsconstraint` needs modification. If the Saint Bernard ran out of food and went to the Black Lab's dish, the Saint Bernard would not be able to eat from it since the levels are not equal (`Dog:large:saint_bernard, black_lab, golden_retriever` is not the same as `dog_chow:large:black_lab`). Remember, the levels are sets, so we need to introduce some notion that if the subjects set dominates the target set, that interaction should be allowed.

This could be accomplished with the `dom` keyword:

```
mlsconstrain food eat (l1 dom l2);
```

The dominate keyword, `dom`, differs from equality, indicating `l1` is a superset of `l2` In other words, the levels associated with the target, `l2`, are among the potentially larger set of levels associated with the subject, `l1`. At this point, we are able to keep all the food separated and used however we see fit.

After getting all these dogs, you realize it's time to feed them, so you get a bag of dog food and put some in each bowl. However, before you can add dog food to the bowls, we need some allow rules and labels that will let you. Remember, SELinux is a whitelist-based system, and everything must be explicitly allowed.

We will label the human with the `human` label and define some rules. Oh yeah... don't forget to feed the cat, as well:

```
allow human dog_chow:food put;
allow human cat_chow:food put;
```

We will also need to label human with all the sensitivities and categories, but this would become cumbersome when we need to add additional dogs, breeds, and breed sizes to our system. We could just bypass the constraint if the type is human. With this approach, we always trust human to put the correct food in the appropriate bowl:

```
mlsconstrain food eat (l1 dom l2);
mlsconstrain food put (t1 == human);
```

Note the addition of put in the access vectors of the MLS constraint. Viola! The human can now feed his ever-growing pack of animals.

So your birthday rolls around, and you receive an automatic dog feeder as a present. You label the food dispenser, dispenser and modify the MLS constraints:

```
mlsconstrain food eat (l1 dom l2);
mlsconstrain food put (t1 == human or t1 == dispenser);
```

Again, we see a need to condense the number of types and get organized to prevent having to duplicate lines. This is where attributes are quite handy. We can assign an attribute to our human and dispenser types by first defining the attribute:

```
attribute feeder;
```

Then we can add it to the type:

```
typeattribute human, feeder;
typeattribute dispenser, feeder;
```

This could also be done at type declaration:

```
type human, feeder;
type dispenser, feeder;
```

At this point, we could modify the MLS statements to look like this:

```
mlsconstrain food eat (l1 dom l2);
mlsconstrain food put (t1 == feeder);
```

Now let's suppose you hire a maid service. You want to ensure anyone sent by the maid service is able to feed your pets. For that matter, let's let your family members feed them, as well. This would be a good use case for the user capabilities. We will define the following users: adults_u, kids_u, and maid_u. Then we'll need to add a constraint statement to allow interactions by these users:

```
mlsconstrain food put (u1 == adults_u or u1 == maid_u);
```

This would prevent the kids from feeding the dogs, but let the maids and adults feed them. Now suppose you hire a gardener. You could create yet another user, `gardener_u`, or you could collapse the users into a few classes and use roles. Let's suppose we collapse `gardener_u` and `maid_u` into `staff_u`. There is no reason the gardener should be feeding the dog, so we could use role-based transitions to move the staff between their duties. For instance, suppose staff can perform more than one service, that is, the same person might garden and clean. In this case, they might take on the role of `gardener_r` or `maid_r`. We could use the role capability of SELinux to meet this need:

```
mlsconstrain food put (u1 == adults_u or (u1 == staff_u and r1 == animal_
care_r);
```

Staff may only feed the dogs when they're in the `animal_care_r` role. How to get into and back out of that role is really the only component missing. You need to have a well-defined system for how the staff can move into the animal care role and transition back out. These transitions in SELinux occur either automatically via dynamic role transitions or via source code modifications. We'll assume that any human entity (gardener, adults, kids) all start in the `human_r` role.

Dynamic role transitions work with a two-part rule, the first part allows the transition to occur via an allow rule:

```
allow human_r animal_care_r;
```

The role transition statements are as follows:

```
role_transition human_r dog_chow animal_care_r;
role_transition human_r cat_chow animal_care_r;
```

This would be a good case to attribute the `dog_chow` and `cat_chow` types to a new attribute, `animal_chow`, and rewrite the preceding role transitions to:

```
typeattribute dog_chow, animal_chow;
typeattribute cat_chow, animal_chow;
role_transition human_r animal_chow animal_care_r;
```

With these role transitions, you can only go from the `human_r` role to `animal_care_r`. You would need to define transitions to get back as well. It's also important to note that you might define other roles. Suppose you define the role `gardener_r`, and when someone is in that role, they cannot transition to `animal_care_r`. Suppose your justification for this policy is that gardeners might work with chemicals unsafe for pets, so they would need to wash their hands before feeding pets. In such a situation, they should only be able to transition to `animal_care_r` from the `hand_wash_r` role.

Complexities and best practices

As you can now appreciate, SELinux is complex, and can be thought of as a general purpose "meta programming policy language". You're literally programming what interactions are allowed to occur in a very complex OS such as Linux, where the interactions themselves are often complex. Just like a programming language, you can do things with different styles and methods that will yield differing results. Perhaps using a `switch()` in that program will make it cleaner and easier to understand rather than an `else-if` block, even though functionally you will end up with the same thing. SELinux is the same; you can often accomplish things with one portion of the enforcement mechanisms that would be more appropriately accomplished using an alternate mechanism. In later chapters, we will cover the process of labeling the target and subject, one of the more difficult parts of the system.

When someone authors a program, they often have a set of requirements in place that the software should perform. These are the requirements of the software. In SELinux, you should do the same thing. You should gather the security requirements and understand the threat models you wish to protect yourself from. A well designed SELinux policy would meet these goals. A great design would do it in a way that is easy to extend. That's ultimately where careful and judicious use of the combination of UBAC, RBAC, TE, and MLS will help achieve the requirements and design goals.

Summary

In this chapter, we covered the major working portions of SELinux that include type enforcement, multilevel and multicategory security, as well as users and roles. Additionally, we saw how to apply these technologies to implement increasingly complex access policies to a tangible example. In the next chapter, we will move outside of the kernel and discover how Android works in its very unique user space.

3
Android Is Weird

It really is. Although it is built on the familiar Linux kernel, Android has a completely custom user space, and while many of its functionalities are rewrites of their GNU cousins, some are either new or have significantly different functions than their desktop counterparts. Because of these differences, these systems had to be modified to support SELinux. In this chapter, we will:

- Introduce the Android security model
- Investigate binder, zygote, and the property service
- Cover which SELinux elements were added to complement these systems and why

The coverage of these systems will be moderate, but we will present more intricate details of each system later, when appropriate, in our exploratory investigation of SE for Android.

Android's security model

Android's core security model is based on Linux DAC, including capabilities. Android, however, uses the Linux concept of UID/GID in a very non-traditional way. Each process on the system has its own UID rather than the UID of whoever launched it. These UIDs (generally unique) provide sandboxing and process isolation. There are a few circumstances, though, where processes can share UIDs and GIDs. Typically, when a process shares a UID with another process, it is because they both need the same set of permissions on the system and share data. The same could be possible for GIDs. However, some GIDs in Android are actually used to gain permission to access underlying systems, such as the SD card filesystem. In a nutshell, the UID is used to isolate processes and not the human users of the system. In fact, Android didn't have support for multiple human users until its Jelly Bean 4.3 release. It was always intended for devices with a single human user… at least in operation.

Within this security model, there are two process classes. The first is called system component services. These are the services declared in the system init scripts. They tend to be highly privileged and thus almost never share a UID with another process. An example system component service would be the **Radio Interface Layer Daemon (RILD)**. RILD is responsible for processing messages between Android userspace and the modem on the device. Because of the nature of what it does, it typically runs as UID root. There is no requirement that processes be pure native code. System server has non-native components, runs as the system UID, and is highly privileged. Almost all of these systems share a common theme; they have a UID that is either root or is set to the owner of many sensitive kernel objects, such as sockets, pipes, and files.

The second class is applications. Applications are typically written in Java, although this is not a requirement; this is similar to how system component services are typically written in native code without it being a requirement. These applications have UIDs assigned automatically when they are installed, and these UIDs are reserved by the system for this purpose. The package manager is responsible for issuing UIDs to applications. These UIDs have no ties to anything sensitive or dangerous on the system, and the applications run with no capabilities. In order to access a system resource, an application must have its supplementary group appended to or it must be arbitrated by a separate process.

A simple example of utilizing the supplementary group is seen when an application needs to use the SD card. For applications to access the SD card, they must have SDCARD_RW in their supplementary GIDs. These permissions are enforced with standard Linux DAC permissions by the kernel. The supplementary group is assigned by the package manager during the application's installation based on a declared permission. Applications in Android must declare something called uses-permission in the application's manifest. This permission appears as a string which is mapped to a supplementary GID. This mapping is maintained in a file in the system, specifically /system/etc/permissions/platform.xml. You will see an application of these permission strings in a later chapter.

The second way an application gains access to a system resource is through another process. The application wishing to use a system resource must get another process to do this on its behalf. Most requests are handled by a process known as the **system server**. The system server checks whether the application making the arbitration request had declared a matching permission string in its manifest file. If it did, it's allowed to proceed, otherwise a security exception is thrown. Even arbitrated accesses in Android use a DAC model, in essence. While the object owner controls the access rules on the object via permission strings, any consumer of the protected object can just request the permission string to get access. Essentially, anyone can write an application requesting any permission strings they want. While installing an application, the user is presented with the list of permissions requested by the application, which they choose to accept or reject en masse. If the user's intent is to install the application, all requested permissions must be granted. If the user is not careful, they might inadvertently allow that application to access protected objects in a way that can threaten the security of the device, applications, or user data. The owners of the devices should always ensure they are comfortable with the application using the declared permissions.

 For examples or further discussion, refer to `http://developer.android.com/guide/topics/security/permissions.html`.

Binder

The arbitrated access method discussed before requires some form of **Interprocess Communication (IPC)**, and while Android does use Unix domain sockets, it also brings its own IPC mechanism that is used more widely throughout the system. This IPC mechanism is called binder and is the core IPC mechanism in the Android operating system. It has historical relevance from the BeOS and Palm OS implementations of OpenBinder, and since the initial Android development team was comprised of many OpenBinder engineers, binder went with them to Android. However, Android has a complete, from scratch rewrite of the binder code base that is specific to Linux.

 Binder is currently not completely mainstreamed into the Linux kernel, and many of Android's kernel changes are still staged.

There is some controversy around binder and its mainline adoption. Some people argue against the amount of heavy lifting it does within the driver in contrast to competing implementations such as dbus. However, it will likely be a long time before we see the resolution of this debate. Regardless of whether binder stays an Android-specific technology, is mainstreamed in the Linux kernel, or is eventually replaced by another technology in Android, binder is here to stay for the foreseeable future.

Binder's architecture

Binder IPC follows a client/server architecture. A service publishes an interface and clients consume from that interface. Clients can bind to services via one of the two methods: known address or service name.

Each binder interface in the system is known as a binder node. Each binder node has an address. When clients want to use an interface, they must bind to a binder node via this address. This is analogous to browsing a webpage via its IP address. However, unlike an IP address that is usually fixed for long durations of time, the binder address could change based on restarts of the publishing service or on the service startup order at the boot time of the device. The order of processes isn't quite guaranteed, thus the publishing of process services can result in a different binder token (a simple binder object to share among processes) being assigned. Also, this indirection allows the runtime ability to reseat service implementations using just the published service names without the necessity to utilize the token.

The way this redirection functions is similar to how DNS provides the resolution from name to IP address for networked device accesses. Binder has something called the context manager (also known as the service manager). The context manager lives at a fixed node address of 0. Publishing services send a name and a binder token to the context manager, and then, when clients need to find a service by name, they check binder node 0 and resolve the name to the binder token. A binder token is the proper name for this address, or ID, that uniquely addresses a binder interface. After a client binds to the binder object, which is a process that implements the binder interface, the processes then perform binder transactions using a well-established binder protocol. This protocol allows synchronous transactions analog to a method call.

Since binder is a kernel driver, it has some nice features that determine what one can do across the interface. For starters, it allows the transmission of file descriptors. It also manages a thread pool for dispatching service methods. Additionally, it employs an approach referred to as zero copy whereby binder does not copy any of the transaction data between processes... it shares them instead. Binder also affords reference counting of objects and lets services query the client application's Linux credentials like UID, GID, and **Process ID (PID)**. Binder also allows the service and client to know when the other has terminated via its link to death functionality.

Typically in Android, you don't work with binder directly. Instead, you work with a service rather via a service and its **Android Interface Description Language (AIDL)** interface. The final chapter will provide detailed examples of AIDL in practice for our custom SE for Android system, but in the meantime, the following is a simple example of an AIDL interface providing the means for remote processes to execute the `getAccountName()` and `putAccountName()` functions:

```
package com.example.sample;

interface IRemoteInterface {
  String getAccountName();
  boolean putAccountName(in String name);
}
```

The beauty in working with an AIDL interface is that it is used to generate a significant amount of code to manage data and processes that would otherwise have to be done by hand. For example, the following is only a small portion of the code generated from the preceding AIDL sample:

```
@Override public boolean onTransact(int code, android.os.Parcel data,
android.os.Parcel reply, int flags) throws android.os.RemoteException
{
switch (code)
{
case INTERFACE_TRANSACTION:
{
reply.writeString(DESCRIPTOR);
return true;
}
case TRANSACTION_getAccountName:
{
data.enforceInterface(DESCRIPTOR);
java.lang.String _result = this.getAccountName();
reply.writeNoException();
reply.writeString(_result);
return true;
}
case TRANSACTION_putAccountName:
{
data.enforceInterface(DESCRIPTOR);
java.lang.String _arg0;
_arg0 = data.readString();
...
```

Binder and security

The security implications of binder are quite large. You should be able to control who becomes the context manager, as a rogue context manager could compromise the whole system by sending clients to rogue services, rather than the proper ones. Outside of that, you might want to control which clients can bind to which binder objects. Lastly, you might wish to control whether file descriptors can be sent via binder. The binder also has the capability to allow someone to fake credentials over the interface, which is designed to be used for good. For example, some privileged system processes, such as **Activity Manager Service (AMS)**, perform operations on behalf of other processes. The credentials exposed in this kind of masquerading are of the process you are doing the work for, not of the privileged entity. This is analogous to a power of attorney, used when someone is acting on your behalf.

Android's binder IPC mechanism was traditionally controlled with DAC permissions. However, as we saw in *Chapter 1, Linux Access Controls*, these permissions have some flaws. It follows that binder needs to be modified to support SELinux because the binder driver does not otherwise implement hooks to any additional security modules. To do this, a patch was sent to Google by Stephen Smalley implementing these features. The patch implements new hooks for consumers of what is known as the **Linux Security Module (LSM)** framework. This framework allows LSMs such as SELinux to be invoked and then make access decisions. The details of this patch are outside the scope of this book. It suffices that binder was patched, and SELinux can now control its capabilities with MAC.

> Stephen Smalley is a computer security researcher at the Trusted Systems Research organization of the United States **National Security Agency (NSA)** and leads the SE Android project. The patch he sent to Google to modify the binder for SELinux hooks can be viewed at https://android-review.googlesource.com/45984.

Because of the integration of SELinux and binder, SE for Android has an additional class with access vectors (a fancy way of saying, "things it can do.") In previous examples from *Chapter 2, Mandatory Access Controls and SELinux*, the target class is food. Similarly, the SELinux class for binder is binder. It defines the access vectors listed in the following bullets. If you recall, the access vector for food in *Chapter 2, Mandatory Access Controls and SELinux*, was eat. The following access vectors are available for binder:

- impersonate: This creates fake credentials over a binder interface
- call: This binds a client to a binder interface and uses it
- set_context_mgr: This sets the context manager
- transfer: This transfers a file descriptor

Zygote – application spawn

Non-native applications in Android historically make use of the Dalvik **virtual machine (VM)** and run a proprietary byte code called DEX. Applications are also spawned from a common process called zygote through a mechanism called fork and specialize. Zygote itself is a process that has the Dalvik VM and some common classes, such as java.util.*, loaded into the VM. Fork and specialize is the mechanism of going from a zygote to a child process of zygote that executes some application code.

 Versions of Android since Android 4.4 are replacing this with the **Android RunTime (ART)**. It is speculated that Android L will not use the Dalvik VM at all.

The first part of this process involves a socket connection. Zygote listens over this socket for an application's spawn requests. Some of the arguments include the package name of the application that should be loaded and a flag that indicates whether the application is the system server or not. Once the spawn command is received, the fork can proceed.

 A great way to start tracing back this initial socket connection is with the app_process tool. This command starts a process with Dalvik. For more information, navigate to frameworks/base/cmds/app_process/app_main.cpp.

After the fork, the now parent zygote returns to listen on the socket for more requests. The child process is executing and a few things need to happen. The first thing that needs to happen is a UID and GID switch. Zygote runs with the UID root, and thus to meet the Android security model, it must set the child process UIDs and GIDs to something other than root. The child process will set UID and GID as defined by the package manager and the supplementary GIDs. It also sets the process' resource limits and scheduling policy. Then it clears the capability set of the application to zero (no capabilities). In the case of the system server, the capability set is not cleared but rather set as one of the arguments sent over the socket. After this point, the child process runs. Code further along in the zygote loads the class, and other system interactions, such as intent delivery, are used to start an activity. These parts of zygote are beyond the scope of this book.

The property service

The property service in Android provides a shared mapping of key-value pairs between all processes. All processes on an Android system share some pages of memory dedicated to this system. However, the mapping in all processes is READ ONLY with the exception of init processes, which have a READ/WRITE mapping. The property service system resides within init, and it is this system's job to update or add values to this key-value map. In order to change a value, you must go through property service, but anyone can read a value. It's imperative that if you use property service, you do not store sensitive information. It is primarily intended to be used for small values, not a generic large-value store. What follows is only a very basic introduction to the property service. A thorough investigation will be conducted later.

To set a property, you must send a request using a Unix domain socket to the property service. Property service will then parse the request and set the value if the permissions allow it to do so. Properties have period-delimited segments, like package names, that have permissions assigned to it statically at build time. The permissions and property service code can be found together at system/ core/property_service.c. The arguments expected over this interface include a command, the property name, and the property value. For those who are curious, these are all defined in the structure prop_msg, which is defined in bionic/libc/ include/sys/_system_properties.h. Upon receiving the message, the property service checks the peer socket's credentials against the static map of permissions. If the UID is root, it can write to anything, otherwise it must be a match for either UID or GID. In very new Android versions, or those with the patch applied from https://android-review.googlesource.com/#/c/98428/, both the permission checking and hardcoded DAC have been replaced by SELinux controls.

Since the permission to set a value is controlled by user space using DAC, it follows that the property set mechanisms share the inherent rooting vulnerability flaw. With this in mind, the property service code was augmented in SELinux. Since this is a user space process, it uses the SELinux API through the kernel to program something called a user space object manager. This just means the user space application checks with SELinux in the kernel to ensure it can perform an activity… in this case, set on a property.

Summary

Android has some very unique properties. From its use of the common UID and GID model to promote its security goals, to its custom binder IPC mechanism, these systems have implications on the security and functionality of the device. In the next chapter, these systems will come back into play as we get the UDOO up and running and enable SE for Android on it.

Installation on the UDOO

4

In order to continue our exploration, we will need to get a tangible system in place to work with. In this chapter, we will:

- Build Android 4.3 for the UDOO from source
- Flash an SD card with our boot images
- Get the UDOO running while capturing logs
- Establish an `adb` connection to the UDOO
- Rebuild the kernel with SELinux support
- Verify our SELinux UDOO image works as expected

We will start with the publicly available UDOO Android 4.3 Jelly Bean source code, which can be downloaded from `http://www.udoo.org/downloads/`. It is assumed you have a UDOO and have verified that it is functional. It is recommended you follow the instructions on the UDOO website for getting started with the Android 4.3 prebuilt image as an initial test (for more information, refer to `http://www.udoo.org/getting-started/`).

You will also need an appropriate development system for working with Android and a UDOO, but the details of this are beyond the scope of this chapter. An appendix has been provided detailing the setup of a standard Ubuntu Linux 12.04 system to ensure you have the highest probability of success duplicating the work in this book.

Retrieving the source

Let's start this exercise by downloading the Android 4.3 Jellybean source code from the download links given in the preceding section, and extract the download into a workspace using the following commands:

```
$ mkdir ~/udoo && cd ~/udoo
$ tar -xavf ~/Downloads/UDOO_Android_4.3_Source_v2.0.tar.gz
```

Once this is done, you should review the UDOO documentation and the Android source code building instructions at the following URLs:

- `http://www.elinux.org/UDOO_compile_android_4-2-2_from_sources`
- `http://source.android.com/source/initializing.html`

The instructions provided by the preceding URL discuss how to build Android with Open JDK 7. However, these instructions are for the current release of Android (L preview) and are not 100 percent relevant. For Android 4.3, you must build with Oracle Java 6, which is archived by Oracle and found at `http://www.oracle.com/technetwork/java/javasebusiness/downloads/java-archive-downloads-javase6-419409.html`.

It is assumed that you have a duplicate of the system detailed in the *Appendix*, *The Development Environment*. That appendix, among other things, walks you through the setup of Oracle Java 6 as your only Java instance. However, for those who prefer to work from their existing systems, particularly those with multiple Java SDKs, please keep in mind you will need to ensure your system is using the Oracle Java 6 tools when working through the rest of this book.

Finish setting up your environment by changing to the root of your UDOO source tree and execute the following command:

```
$ . setup udoo-eng
```

Once the environment is configured, we need to build the `bootloader`:

```
$ cd bootable/bootloader/uboot-imx
$ ./compile.sh -c
```

A graphical menu will appear. Ensure the settings are as follows:

- **DDR Size**: Select 1 Giga, bus size 64, and active CS \ 1 (256Mx4)
- **Board Type**: Select UDOO

- **CPU type**: Select quad-core or dual-core option, dependent on which system you have. We happen to be using the quad-core system.
- **OS type**: Select **Android**
- **Environment device**: Must select **SD/MMC**
- **Extra options**: **CLEAN** should be selected
- **Compiler options**: Paths to tool chains can be selected here; just take the defaults

The following screenshot shows the graphical menu displayed by the preceding command:

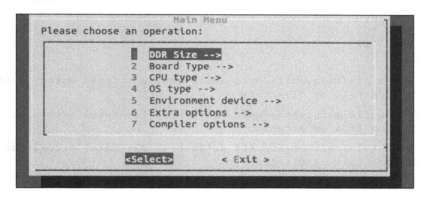

When you exit, be sure to save. Then start the compilation:

```
$ ./compile.sh
Board type selected: UDOO
CPU Type: QUAD/DUAL
OS type: Android
...
/home/bookuser/udoo/prebuilts/gcc/linux-x86/arm/arm-eabi-4.6/bin/arm-
eabi-objcopy -O srec u-boot u-boot.srec
/home/bookuser/udoo/prebuilts/gcc/linux-x86/arm/arm-eabi-4.6/bin/arm-
eabi-objcopy --gap-fill=0xff -O binary u-boot u-boot.bin
```

Just to be safe, verify your build was successful by using `ls u-boot.bin` to ensure the `bootloader` image now exists. Now, build Android using the following command:

```
$ croot
$ make -j4 2>&1 | tee logz
```

The first command is something that was sourced in the setup scripts for Android and takes us back to the root of our project tree. The second command, make, builds the system. You should set the option for j to twice your CPU/core count in most cases. Because many of you might have a dual-core machine, we'll use -j4. One of the authors of this book uses 8 CPU cores, for example, and uses the flag -j16. The file redirection and tee commands capture the build output to a file. This is important to help and debug any build issues. This build, depending on your system can take a long, long time. On the previously mentioned 8-core system with 16GB RAM, this took a little over 35 minutes. On other systems, we've experienced build times over 3 hours.

In this case, capturing the logs proved very useful. The build terminated with an error, and by searching the logs for error, we found the following:

```
$ grep error logz
...
external/mtd-utils/mkfs.ubifs/mkfs.ubifs.h:48:23: fatal error: uuid/
uuid.h: No such file or directory
external/mtd-utils/mkfs.ubifs/mkfs.ubifs.h:48:23: fatal error: uuid/
uuid.h: No such file or directory
external/mtd-utils/mkfs.ubifs/mkfs.ubifs.h:48:23: fatal error: uuid/
uuid.h: No such file or directory
...
```

By evaluating those errors, we discover we are missing headers for uuid and lzo1x. We can also open the Android makefile, external/mtd-utils/mkfs.ubifs/Android.mk, and determine the likely libraries involved from the line LOCAL_LDLIBS:= -lz -llzo2 -lm -luuid -m64. Searching reveals the specific Ubuntu package we're missing; we will install them and build again. The $ character at the end of the search string ensures we only get results ending in uuid/uuid.h. Without it, we might match files ending in .html or .hpp:

```
$ sudo apt-file search -x "uuid/uuid.h$"
uuid-dev: /usr/include/uuid/uuid.h
$ sudo apt-get install uuid-dev
$ make -j4 2>&1 | tee logz
```

A successful build should produce some final output similar to the following:

```
...
```

```
Running: mkuserimg.sh out/target/product/udoo/system out/target/product/
udoo/obj/PACKAGING/systemimage_intermediates/system.img ext4 system
293601280 out/target/product/udoo/root/file_contexts
```

```
Install system fs image: out/target/product/udoo/system.img
```

```
out/target/product/udoo/system.img+out/target/product/udoo/obj/PACKAGING/
recovery_patch_intermediates/recovery_from_boot.p maxsize=299747712
blocksize=4224 total=294120167 reserve=3028608
```

Flashing image on an SD card

With the `bootloader`, Android userspace, and Linux kernel built, it's time to insert an SD card and flash the images. Insert an SD card into your host computer, and ensure it's unmounted. In Ubuntu, removable media are mounted automatically, so you'll need to find the `/dev/sd*` device that is your flash drive, and `umount` it. For the remainder of the text, we will use `/dev/sdd` as the flash drive, but it is important to use the correct device for your system. If you have used this SD card for installing UDOO before, the card will contain multiple partitions, so you might see `/dev/sdd<num>` mounted numerous times:

```
$ mount | grep sdd
/dev/sdd7 on /media/vender type ext4 (rw,nosuid,nodev,uhelper=udisks)
/dev/sdd4 on /media/data type ext4 (rw,nosuid,nodev,uhelper=udisks)
/dev/sdd5 on /media/57f8f4bc-abf4-655f-bf67-946fc0f9f25b type ext4 (rw,no
suid,nodev,uhelper=udisks)
/dev/sdd6 on /media/cache type ext4 (rw,nosuid,nodev,uhelper=udisks)
$ sudo bash -c "umount /dev/sdd4 && umount /dev/sdd5 && umount /dev/sdd6
&& umount /dev/sdd7"
```

Once the SD card is properly unmounted, we can flash our image:

```
$ sudo -E ./make_sd.sh /dev/sdd
```

 You must use the `-E` parameter on `sudo` to preserve all the exported variables from the Android build. You must be in the same terminal session you built Android in. Otherwise you will see the error `No OUT export variable found! Setup not called in advance`....

Once this completes (it will take a while), it's important to flush the block device caches back to the disk with the command, `sudo sync`. Then, you can remove the SD card, insert it into the UDOO, and boot!

UDOO serial and Android Debug Bridge

Now that the UDOO is booting into Android, we want to make sure we can access it using the serial port as well as the **Android Debug Bridge (adb)**. You'll need the UDOO serial drivers appropriate for your system. The details of this for Mac, Linux, and Windows can be found at

http://www.udoo.org/ProjectsAndTutorials/connecting-via-serial-cable/.

The serial port is the first form of communication that will come from the system, and it is initialized by the `bootloader`. It is a critical link for debugging any kernel or system issues that you encounter later on. It's also required in order to configure the USB port to allow `adb` connections across CN3 (the USB OTG port on the UDOO). To configure the port, we need to configure and use minicom to connect a shell to the device. Start by plugging a micro USB cable from CN6 (the micro USB port closest to the power button) to the host machine. Next, let's find the serial connection by looking through `dmesg` for the connection message of a TTY over USB.

```
$ sudo dmesg | tail -n 5
[ 9019.090058] usb 4-1: Manufacturer: Silicon Labs
[ 9019.090061] usb 4-1: SerialNumber: 0078AEDB
[ 9019.096089] cp210x 4-1:1.0: cp210x converter detected
[ 9019.208023] usb 4-1: reset full-speed USB device number 4 using uhci_
hcd
[ 9019.359172] usb 4-1: cp210x converter now attached to ttyUSB0
```

Our TTY terminal is on the last line. Let's connect through it with `minicom`:

```
$ sudo minicom -sw
```

Select **Serial Port Setup**, type `a`, change **Serial Device** to /dev/ttyUSB0, and type `f` to toggle the hardware flow control off:

To exit, hit *Enter*, select **Save Setup and DFL**, then select **Exit from Minicom**, and press *Enter*. Now run `minicom` to connect to your UDOO, and watch it boot:

```
$ sudo minicom -w
```

If the device is booted and running, you'll get a friendly root shell:

```
Welcome to minicom 2.5

OPTIONS: I18n
Compiled on May  2 2011, 10:05:24.
Port /dev/ttyUSB0

Press CTRL-A Z for help on special keys


127|root@udoo:/ # AT S7=45 S0=0 L1 V1 X4 &c1 E1 Q0
[1] 3584
/system/bin/sh: c1: not found
/system/bin/sh: AT: not found
127|root@udoo:/ #
```

If it's booting, you'll see the logs. Just wait for the root shell prompt:

```
U-Boot 2009.08 (Sep 08 2014 - 17:29:49)

CPU: Freescale i.MX6 family TO1.2 at 792 MHz
Thermal sensor with ration = 181
Temperature:   43 C, calibration data 0x5774e269
mx6q pll1: 792MHz
mx6q pll2: 528MHz
mx6q pll3: 480MHz
mx6q pll4: 50MHz
ipg clock       : 66000000Hz
ipg per clock   : 66000000HZ
uart clock      : 80000000Hz
cspi clock      : 60000000Hz
ahb clock       : 132000000Hz
axi clock    : 264000000Hz
emi_slow clock: 132000000Hz
ddr clock       : 528000000Hz
usdhc1 clock    : 198000000Hz
usdhc2 clock    : 198000000Hz
usdhc3 clock    : 198000000Hz
usdhc4 clock    : 198000000Hz
nfc clock       : 240000000Hz
Board: i.MX6Q-UDOO: unknown-board Board: 0x63012
```

Now we need to flip some GPIO pins to move the CN3 micro USB into debug mode:

```
root@udoo:/ # echo 0 > /sys/class/gpio/gpio203/value
root@udoo:/ # echo 0 > /sys/class/gpio/gpio128/value
```

Then, reset the SAM3X8E processor that was using that bus, by removing and replacing the J16 jumper. Now plug in a micro USB cable from the host to CN3. You should now see a USB device as well as `adb`:

```
$ lsusb
Bus 001 Device 009: ID 18d1:4e42 Google Inc.
$ adb devices
List of devices attached
0123456789ABCDEF   offline
```

You need to select **Allow USB debugging** when the prompt appears on the UDOO Android side. When you do this, the device should go from offline to online; this way you can use `adb`.

Now test the connection and grab the screenshot over `adb`:

```
$ adb shell
root@udoo:/ #
$ adb shell screencap -p | perl -pe 's/\x0D\x0A/\x0A/g' > screen.png
```

This is the screenshot:

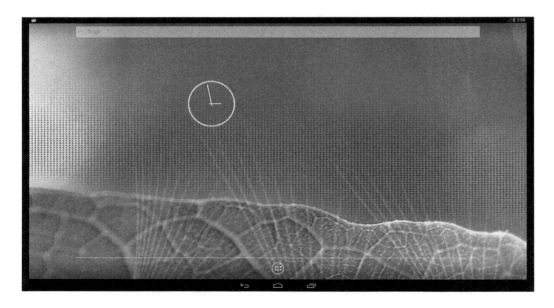

At this point, we have a working development system. We have early boot logs and a rescue shell through the serial console. We also have an `adb` bridge with which we can use the standard Android debugging tools! There's nothing left to do but get this system secured with SELinux!

Flipping the switch

Now that we are enabling SELinux on the UDOO, we need to verify it isn't turned on. The way to do this is to check the known `filesystem` types in the `/proc` filesystem. SELinux has its own psuedo-filesystem, so if it's enabled, we should see it in the list:

```
$ adb shell cat /proc/filesystems
nodev    sysfs
nodev    rootfs
nodev    bdev
nodev    proc
nodev    cgroup
nodev    cpuset
nodev    tmpfs
nodev    debugfs
nodev    sockfs
nodev    pipefs
nodev    anon_inodefs
nodev    rpc_pipefs
nodev    devpts
         ext3
         ext2
         ext4
         cramfs
nodev    ramfs
         vfat
         msdos
nodev    nfs
nodev    jffs2
nodev    fuse
         fuseblk
nodev    fusectl
nodev    mtd_inodefs
nodev    ubifs
```

There is no evidence of SELinux here, so let's find the kernel configuration and turn it on. Execute this command from the ~/udoo/kernel_imx directory, and eventually you will be greeted with a graphical editing screen:

```
$ make menuconfig
```

First, you will need to enable **Auditing support**, as this is a dependency of SELinux. Under **General setup | Auditing Support**, enable **Audit Support** and **Enable system-call auditing**. Use the up and down arrow keys to highlight an entry, and press the spacebar to enable it. When an item is enabled, you will see an asterisk (*) next to it:

```
                              General setup
Arrow keys navigate the menu.  <Enter> selects submenus --->.  Highlighted letters are hotkeys.
Pressing <Y> includes, <N> excludes, <M> modularizes features.  Press <Esc><Esc> to exit, <?>
for Help, </> for Search.  Legend: [*] built-in  [ ] excluded  <M> module  < > module capable

      [*] System V IPC
      [ ] POSIX Message Queues
      [ ] BSD Process Accounting
      [ ] open by fhandle syscalls
      [ ] Export task/process statistics through netlink (EXPERIMENTAL)
      [*] Auditing support
          IRQ subsystem  --->
          RCU Subsystem  --->
      <*> Kernel .config support
      [*]    Enable access to .config through /proc/config.gz

                <Select>    < Exit >    < Help >
```

Go back to the main menu by selecting **Exit**... it's not very intuitive. Enter the **File systems** menu, and for each of the three filesystems, **Ext2**, **Ext3**, and **Ext4**, ensure that **Extended attributes** and **Security Labels** are enabled. Then, go back to the main menu by selecting **Exit**:

```
                              File systems
Arrow keys navigate the menu.  <Enter> selects submenus --->.  Highlighted letters are hotkeys.
Pressing <Y> includes, <N> excludes, <M> modularizes features.  Press <Esc><Esc> to exit, <?>
for Help, </> for Search.  Legend: [*] built-in  [ ] excluded  <M> module  < > module capable

      <*> Second extended fs support
      [*]    Ext2 extended attributes
      [ ]       Ext2 POSIX Access Control Lists
      [*]       Ext2 Security Labels
      [ ]    Ext2 execute in place support
      <*> Ext3 journalling file system support
      [ ]    Default to 'data=ordered' in ext3
      [*]    Ext3 extended attributes
      [ ]       Ext3 POSIX Access Control Lists
      [*]       Ext3 Security Labels
      <*> The Extended 4 (ext4) filesystem
      [*]    Ext4 extended attributes
      [ ]       Ext4 POSIX Access Control Lists
      [*]       Ext4 Security Labels
      [ ]    EXT4 debugging support
      [ ] JBD (ext3) debugging support

                <Select>    < Exit >    < Help >
```

From that screen, exit back to the main menu and go to **Security Options**. Once in the **Security Options** submenu, enable the **Enable different security models** and **Socket and Networking Security Hooks** options:

```
[*]  Enable different security models
[ ]  Enable the securityfs filesystem
[*]  Socket and Networking Security Hooks
[ ]    XFRM (IPSec) Networking Security Hooks (NEW)
```

Once these are enabled, more options will appear. Enable **NSA SELinux Support** and ensure the other selections and values from the following screenshot are duplicated:

```
[*]  NSA SELinux Support
[ ]      NSA SELinux boot parameter (NEW)
[ ]      NSA SELinux runtime disable (NEW)
[*]      NSA SELinux Development Support (NEW)
[*]      NSA SELinux AVC Statistics (NEW)
(1)      NSA SELinux checkreqprot default value (NEW)
[*]      NSA SELinux maximum supported policy format version
(23)       NSA SELinux maximum supported policy format version value
```

Finally, set **Default security module** to SELinux:

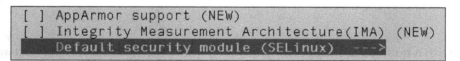

```
[ ]  AppArmor support (NEW)
[ ]  Integrity Measurement Architecture(IMA) (NEW)
     Default security module (SELinux)   --->
```

Once you select **Default security module**, a new window will appear from which you can select **SELinux**. Exit the configuration menus by selecting **Exit** until you are asked to save your new configuration:

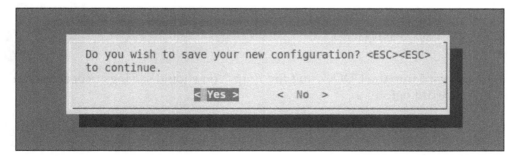

```
Do you wish to save your new configuration? <ESC><ESC>
to continue.

            < Yes >        <  No  >
```

Save the new configuration and write these changes to the originating kernel configuration file. Otherwise, it will be overwritten on subsequent builds. To do this, we'll need to discover which configuration file was used in the default build, which we built earlier before we made our own configuration with make menuconfig:

```
$ grep defconfig logz make -C kernel_imx imx6_udoo_android_defconfig
ARCH=arm CROSS_COMPILE=`pwd`/prebuilts/gcc/linux-x86/arm/arm-eabi-4.6/
bin/arm-eabi-
```

You can see that imx6_udoo_android_defconfig was used as the default configuration. Copy your custom configuration and build again:

```
$ cp .config arch/arm/configs/imx6_udoo_android_defconfig
$ croot
$ make –j4 bootimage 2>&1 | tee logz
```

A quick sanity check of the log file is always a good idea to verify SELinux was actually built into the kernel:

```
$ grep -i selinux logz
HOSTCC scripts/selinux/mdp/mdp
HOSTCC scripts/selinux/genheaders/genheaders
GEN security/selinux/flask.h security/selinux/av_permissions.h
CC security/selinux/avc.o
...
```

Now, with a built kernel supporting SELinux, insert the SD card into the host and run the following commands:

```
$ sudo -E ./make_sd.sh /dev/sdd
$ sudo sync
```

> Don't forget to umount any automounted partitions from the SD card as we did before.

Plug the SD card into the UDOO, and fire it up. You should see logs over the serial console as we did before:

```
U-Boot 2009.08 (Sep 08 2014 - 21:56:36)

CPU: Freescale i.MX6 family TO1.2 at 792 MHz
Thermal sensor with ration = 181
Temperature:   43 C, calibration data 0x5774e269
mx6q pll1:  792MHz
mx6q pll2:  528MHz
mx6q pll3:  480MHz
mx6q pll4:  50MHz
```

Eventually, the serial connection should take us to a root shell.

It's alive

How do we know that we have successfully enabled SELinux in the kernel? Earlier in this chapter, you ran the command, adb shell cat /proc/filesystems. We're going to do the same thing and look for a new filesystem called selinuxfs. If that is present, it indicates we have enabled SELinux successfully. Run the following command in the serial terminal:

```
# cat /proc/filesystems | grep selinux
nodev selinuxfs
```

We can see that selinuxfs is present! Another common practice is to check dmesg for any SELinux output. To do this, execute the following command via the serial terminal:

```
# dmesg | grep -i selinux
<6>SELinux: Initializing.
<7>SELinux: Starting in permissive mode
<7>SELinux: Registering netfilter hooks
<3>SELinux: policydb version 26 does not match my version range 15-23
<4>SELinux: Could not load policy: Invalid argument
```

Summary

This was a very exciting chapter. You learned how to enable SELinux in the kernel configuration, boot the "secured" system, and how to verify its presence. We also learned how to flash and build images for the UDOO in general and how to connect to it via serial and adb connections. In the next chapters, we will focus on how to make the UDOO usable with SE for Android capabilities.

5
Booting the System

Now that we have an SE for Android system, we need to see how we can make use of it, and get it into a usable state. In this chapter, we will:

- Modify the log level to gain more details while debugging
- Follow the boot process relative to the policy loader
- Investigate SELinux APIs and SELinuxFS
- Correct issues with the maximum policy version number
- Apply patches to load and verify an NSA policy

You might have noticed some disturbing error messages in dmesg in *Chapter 4, Installation on the UDOO*. To refresh your memory, here are some of them:

```
# dmesg | grep -i selinux
<6>SELinux: Initializing.
<7>SELinux: Starting in permissive mode
<7>SELinux: Registering netfilter hooks
<3>SELinux: policydb version 26 does not match my version range 15-23
...
```

It would appear that even though SELinux is enabled, we don't quite have an error-free system. At this point, we need to understand what causes this error, and what we can do to rectify it. At the end of this chapter, we should be able to identify the boot process of an SE for Android device with respect to policy loading, and how that policy is loaded into the kernel. We will then address the policy version error.

Policy load

An Android device follows a boot sequence similar to that of the *NIX booting sequence. The boot loader boots the kernel, and the kernel finally executes the init process. The init process is responsible for managing the boot process of the device through init scripts and some hard coded logic in the daemon. Like all processes, init has an entry point at the main function. This is where the first userspace process begins. The code can be found by navigating to `system/core/init/init.c`.

When the init process enters `main` (refer to the following code excerpt), it processes `cmdline`, mounts some `tmpfs` filesystems such as `/dev`, and some pseudo-filesystems such as `procfs`. For SE for Android devices, init was modified to load the policy into the kernel as early in the boot process as possible. The policy in an SELinux system is not built into the kernel; it resides in a separate file. In Android, the only filesystem mounted in early boot is the root filesystem, a ramdisk built into `boot.img`. The policy can be found in this root filesystem at `/sepolicy` on the UDOO or target device. At this point, the init process calls a function to load the policy from the disk and sends it to the kernel, as follows:

```
int main(int argc, char *argv[]) {
...
  process_kernel_cmdline();
  unionselinux_callback cb;
  cb.func_log = klog_write;
  selinux_set_callback(SELINUX_CB_LOG, cb);

  cb.func_audit = audit_callback;
  selinux_set_callback(SELINUX_CB_AUDIT, cb);

  INFO("loading selinux policy\n");
  if (selinux_enabled) {
    if (selinux_android_load_policy() < 0) {
      selinux_enabled = 0;
      INFO("SELinux: Disabled due to failed policy load\n");
    } else {
      selinux_init_all_handles();
    }
  } else {
    INFO("SELinux:  Disabled by command line option\n");
  }
...
```

In the preceding code, you will notice the very nice log message, `SELinux: Disabled due to failed policy load`, and wonder why we didn't see this when we ran `dmesg` before. This code executes before `setlevel` in `init.rc` is executed.

The default init log level is set by the definition of KLOG_DEFAULT_LEVEL in system/core/include/cutils/klog.h. If we really wanted to, we could change that, rebuild, and actually see that message.

Now that we have identified the initial path of the policy load, let's follow it on its course through the system. The selinux_android_load_policy() function can be found in the Android fork of libselinux, which is in the UDOO Android source tree. The library can be found at external/libselinux, and all of the Android modifications can be found in src/android.c.

The function starts by mounting a pseudo-filesystem called **SELinuxFS**. If you recall, this was one of the new filesystems mentioned in /proc/filesystems that we saw in *Chapter 4, Installation on the UDOO*. In systems that do not have sysfs mounted, the mount point is /selinux; on systems that have sysfs mounted, the mount point is /sys/fs/selinux.

You can check mountpoints on a running system using the following command:

```
# mount | grep selinuxfs
selinuxfs /sys/fs/selinux selinuxfs rw,relatime 0 0
```

SELinuxFS is an important filesystem as it provides the interface between the kernel and userspace for controlling and manipulating SELinux. As such, it has to be mounted for the policy load to work. The policy load uses the filesystem to send the policy file bytes to the kernel. This happens in the selinux_android_load_policy() function:

```
int selinux_android_load_policy(void)
{
  char *mnt = SELINUXMNT;
  int rc;
  rc = mount(SELINUXFS, mnt, SELINUXFS, 0, NULL);
  if (rc < 0) {
    if (errno == ENODEV) {
      /* SELinux not enabled in kernel */
      return -1;
    }
    if (errno == ENOENT) {
      /* Fall back to legacy mountpoint. */
      mnt = OLDSELINUXMNT;
      rc = mkdir(mnt, 0755);
      if (rc == -1 && errno != EEXIST) {
        selinux_log(SELINUX_ERROR,"SELinux:
          Could not mkdir:  %s\n",
        strerror(errno));
```

```
        return -1;
      }
      rc = mount(SELINUXFS, mnt, SELINUXFS, 0, NULL);
    }
  }
  if (rc < 0) {
    selinux_log(SELINUX_ERROR,"SELinux:  Could not mount
selinuxfs:  %s\n",
    strerror(errno));
    return -1;
  }
  set_selinuxmnt(mnt);

  return selinux_android_reload_policy();
}
```

The set_selinuxmnt(car *mnt) function changes a global variable in libselinux so that other routines can find the location of this vital interface. From there it calls another helper function, selinux_android_reload_policy(), which is located in the same libselinux android.c file. It loops through an array of possible policy locations in priority order. This array is defined as follows:

```
Static const char *const sepolicy_file[] = {
  "/data/security/current/sepolicy",
  "/sepolicy",
  0 };
```

Since only the root filesystem is mounted, it chooses /sepolicy at this time. The other path is for dynamic runtime reloads of policy. After acquiring a valid file descriptor to the policy file, the system is memory mapped into its address space, and calls security_load_policy(map, size) to load it to the kernel. This function is defined in load_policy.c. Here, the map parameter is the pointer to the beginning of the policy file, and the size parameter is the size of the file in bytes:

```
int selinux_android_reload_policy(void)
{
  int fd = -1, rc;
  struct stat sb;
  void *map = NULL;
  int i = 0;

  while (fd < 0 && sepolicy_file[i]) {
    fd = open(sepolicy_file[i], O_RDONLY | O_NOFOLLOW);
    i++;
  }
```

```
if (fd < 0) {
    selinux_log(SELINUX_ERROR, "SELinux:  Could not open
sepolicy:  %s\n",
    strerror(errno));
    return -1;
}
if (fstat(fd, &sb) < 0) {
    selinux_log(SELINUX_ERROR, "SELinux:  Could not stat %s:  %s\n",
    sepolicy_file[i], strerror(errno));
    close(fd);
    return -1;
}
map = mmap(NULL, sb.st_size, PROT_READ, MAP_PRIVATE, fd, 0);
if (map == MAP_FAILED) {
    selinux_log(SELINUX_ERROR, "SELinux:  Could not map %s:  %s\n",
    sepolicy_file[i], strerror(errno));
    close(fd);
    return -1;
}

rc = security_load_policy(map, sb.st_size);
if (rc < 0) {
    selinux_log(SELINUX_ERROR, "SELinux:  Could not load
policy:  %s\n",
    strerror(errno));
    munmap(map, sb.st_size);
    close(fd);
    return -1;
}

munmap(map, sb.st_size);
close(fd);
selinux_log(SELINUX_INFO, "SELinux: Loaded policy from %s\n",
sepolicy_file[i]);

    return 0;
}
```

The security load policy opens the <selinuxmnt>/load file, which in our case is /sys/fs/selinux/load. At this point, the policy is written to the kernel via this pseudo file:

```
int security_load_policy(void *data, size_t len)
{
    char path[PATH_MAX];
```

```
    int fd, ret;

    if (!selinux_mnt) {
      errno = ENOENT;
      return -1;
    }

    snprintf(path, sizeof path, "%s/load", selinux_mnt);
    fd = open(path, O_RDWR);
    if (fd < 0)
    return -1;

    ret = write(fd, data, len);
    close(fd);
    if (ret < 0)
    return -1;
    return 0;
}
```

Fixing the policy version

At this point, we have a clear idea of how the policy is loaded into the kernel. This is very important. SELinux integration with Android began in Android 4.0, so when porting to various forks and fragments, this breaks, and code is often missing. Understanding all parts of the system, however cursory, will help us to correct issues as they appear in the wild and develop. This information is also useful to understand the system as a whole, so when modifications need to be made, you'll know where to look and how things work. At this point, we're ready to correct the policy versions.

The logs and kernel config are clear; only policy versions up to 23 are supported, and we're trying to load policy version 26. This will probably be a common problem with Android considering kernels are often out of date.

There is also an issue with the 4.3 sepolicy shipped by Google. Some changes by Google made it a bit more difficult to configure devices as they tailored the policy to meet their release goals. Essentially, the policy allows nearly everything and therefore generates very few denial logs. Some domains in the policy are completely permissive via a per-domain permissive statement, and those domains also have rules to allow everything so denial logs do not get generated. To correct this, we can use a more complete policy from the NSA. Replace external/sepolicy with the download from https://bitbucket.org/seandroid/external-sepolicy/get/seandroid-4.3.tar.bz2.

After we extract the NSA's policy, we need to correct the policy version. The policy is located in `external/sepolicy` and is compiled with a tool called `check_policy`. The `Android.mk` file for sepolicy will have to pass this version number to the compiler, so we can adjust this here. On the top of the file, we find the culprit:

```
. . .
# Must be <= /selinux/policyvers reported by the Android kernel.
# Must be within the compatibility range reported by checkpolicy -V.
POLICYVERS ?= 26
. . .
```

Since the variable is overridable by the `?=` assignment. We can override this in `BoardConfig.mk`. Edit `device/fsl/imx6/BoardConfigCommon.mk`, adding the following `POLICYVERS` line to the bottom of the file:

```
. . .
BOARD_FLASH_BLOCK_SIZE := 4096
TARGET_RECOVERY_UI_LIB := librecovery_ui_imx
# SELinux Settings
POLICYVERS := 23
-include device/google/gapps/gapps_config.mk
```

Since the policy is on the `boot.img` image, build the policy and `bootimage`:

```
$ mmm -B external/sepolicy/
$ make -j4 bootimage 2>&1 | tee logz
!!!!!!!!! WARNING !!!!!!!!!! VERIFY BLOCK DEVICE !!!!!!!!!!
$ sudo chmod 666 /dev/sdd1
$ dd if=$OUT/boot.img of=/dev/sdd1 bs=8192 conv=fsync
```

Eject the SD card, place it into the UDOO, and boot.

The first of the preceding commands should produce the following log output:

```
out/host/linux-x86/bin/checkpolicy: writing binary
representation (version 23) to out/target/product/udoo/
obj/ETC/sepolicy_intermediates/sepolicy
```

At this point, by checking the SELinux logs using dmesg, we can see the following:

```
# dmesg | grep -i selinux
<6>init: loading selinux policy
<7>SELinux: 128 avtab hash slots, 490 rules.
<7>SELinux: 128 avtab hash slots, 490 rules.
<7>SELinux: 1 users, 2 roles, 274 types, 0 bools, 1 sens, 1024 cats
<7>SELinux: 84 classes, 490 rules
<7>SELinux: Completing initialization.
```

Another command we need to run is getenforce. The getenforce command gets the SELinux enforcing status. It can be in one of three states:

- **Disabled**: No policy is loaded or there is no kernel support
- **Permissive**: Policy is loaded and the device logs denials (but is not in enforcing mode)
- **Enforcing**: This state is similar to the permissive state except that policy violations result in EACCESS being returned to userspace

One of the goals while booting an SELinux system is to get to the enforcing state. Permissive is used for debugging, as follows:

```
# getenforce
Permissive
```

Summary

In this chapter, we covered the important policy load flow through the init process. We also changed the policy version to suit our development efforts and kernel version. From there, we were able to load the NSA policy and verify that the system loaded it. This chapter additionally showcased some of the SELinux APIs and their interactions with SELinuxFS. In the next chapter, we will examine the filesystem and then move forward in our quest to get the system into enforcing mode.

6
Exploring SELinuxFS

In the last few chapters, we saw SELinuxFS surface on numerous occasions. From its entry in /proc/filesystems to the policy load in the init daemon, it sees frequent use in an SELinux-enabled system. SELinuxFS is the kernel-to-userspace interface and the foundation on which higher userspace idioms and libselinux are built. In this chapter, we will explore the capabilities of this filesystem for a deeper understanding of how the system works. Specifically, we will:

- Determine how to find the mount point of the SELinux filesystem
- Extract status information about our current SELinux system
- Modify our SELinux system status on the fly from the shell and through code
- Investigate ProcFS interfaces

Locating the filesystem

The first thing we need to do is locate the mount point for the filesystem. libselinux mounts the filesystem in either of two places: /selinux (by default) or /sys/fs/selinux. However, this is not a strict requirement and can be altered with a call to void set_selinuxmnt(char *mnt), which sets the SELinux mount point location. However, this should happen without intervention and should not need any adjustment in most circumstances.

The best way to find the mount point in the system is by running the mount command and finding the location of the filesystem. From the serial console, issue the following commands:

```
root@udoo:/ # mount | grep selinux
selinuxfs /sys/fs/selinux selinuxfs rw,relatime 0 0
```

As you can see, the mount point is `/sys/fs/selinux`. Let's go to that directory by issuing the following command at the serial terminal prompt:

```
root@udoo:/ # cd /sys/fs/selinux
root@udoo:/sys/fs/selinux #
```

You are now in the root of the SELinux filesystem.

Interrogating the filesystem

You can interrogate SELinuxFS to find out what the kernel's highest supported policy version is. This is useful when you begin to work with systems you did not build from source. It is also useful when you do not have direct access to the KConfig file. It is important to note that both DAC and MAC permissions apply to this filesystem. With respect to MAC and SELinux, the access vectors for this are enumerated in class security in the policy file located at `external/sepolicy/access_vectors`:

```
root@udoo:/sys/fs/selinux # echo 'cat policyvers'
23
```

 In the previous command, and in several commands to follow, we do not just print the files with the `cat` command. This is because these files do not have a trailing newline at the end of the file. Without the newline, the command prompt following the command's execution would be at the end of the last line of the output. Wrapping the `cat` command with `echo` guarantees a newline. An alternate way to get the same effect is by using `cat policyvers ; echo`.

As we expected, the supported version is 23. As you recall, we set this value in *Chapter 4, Installation on the UDOO* while configuring the kernel to enable SELinux using `make menuconfig` from the `kernel_imx` directory. This is also accessible by the `libselinux` API:

```
int security_policyvers(void);
```

It should not require any elevated permissions and is readable by anyone on the system.

The enforce node

In previous chapters, we discussed that SELinux operates in two modes, **enforcing** and **permissive**. Both modes log policy violations, however, enforcing mode causes the kernel to deny access to the resource and return an error to the calling userspace process (for example, EACCESS). SELinuxFS has an interface to query this status — the file node enforce. Reading from this file returns the status 0 or 1 depending on whether we are running in permissive or enforcing mode, respectively:

```
root@udoo:/sys/fs/selinux # echo 'cat enforce'
0
```

As you can see, our system is in permissive mode. Android has a toolbox command for printing this as well. This command returns the status Permissive or Enforcing depending on whether we are running in a permissive or enforcing mode, respectively:

```
root@udoo:/sys/fs/selinux # getenforce
Permissive
```

You can also write to the enforce file. The DAC permissions for this filesystem are:

```
Owner: root read, write
Group: root read
Others: read
```

Anyone can get the enforcing status, but to set it, you must be the root user. The MAC permission required for this is:

```
class: security
vector: setenforce
```

A command called setenforce can change the status:

```
root@udoo:/sys/fs/selinux # setenforce 0
```

To see what the command does, run it in `strace`:

```
root@udoo:/sys/fs/selinux # strace setenforce 0


...
open("/proc/self/task/3275/attr/current", O_RDONLY) = 4
brk(0x41d80000) = 0x41d80000
read(4, "u:r:init_shell:s0\0", 4095) = 18
close(4) = 0
open("/sys/fs/selinux/enforce", O_RDWR) = 4
write(4, "0", 1)
...
```

As we can see, the interface to `enforce` is as simple as writing 0 or 1. The function in `libselinux` to do this is `int security_setenforce(int value)`. Another interesting artifact of the preceding command is we can see `procfs` was accessed. SELinux has some additional entries in `procfs` as well. Those will be covered further in this chapter.

The disable file interface

SELinux can also be disabled at runtime using the `disable` file interface. However, the kernel must be built with `CONFIG_SECURITY_SELINUX_DISABLE=y`. Our kernel was not built with this option. This file is write only by owner and has no specific MAC permission associated with it. We recommend keeping this option disabled. Additionally, SELinux can be disabled before a policy is loaded. Even when the option is enabled, once a policy is loaded, it is disabled.

The policy file

The `policy` file lets you read the current SELinux policy file that was loaded into the kernel. This can be read and saved to disk:

```
root@udoo:/sys/fs/selinux # cat policy > /sdcard/policy
```

By enabling the `adb` interface, you can now extract it from the device and analyze it on the host with the standard SELinux tools. The DAC permissions on this file are owner: `root`, `read`. There is no SELinux permission specific to this file.

The inverse to the `policy` file is the `load` file. We have seen this file appear when the policy file is loaded by init using the `libselinux` API:

```
int security_load_policy(void *data, size_t len);
```

The null file

The null file is used by SELinux to redirect unauthorized file accesses when domain transitions occur. Remember that a domain transition is when you transition from one context to another. In most cases, this occurs when a program performs a fork and exec function, but this could happen programmatically. In either case, the process has file references it can no longer access, and to help keep processes from crashing, they just write/read from the SELinux null device.

The mls file

One of the capabilities our system has is that our current policy is using **multilevel security (MLS)** support. This is either 0 or 1, based on whether the loaded policy file is using it. Since we have it enabled, we would expect to see 1 from this file:

```
root@udoo:/sys/fs/selinux # echo 'cat mls'
1
```

The mls file is readable by all and has a corresponding SELinux API:

```
int is_selinux_mls_enabled(void)
```

The status file

The version file allows a mechanism by which you can be informed of updates that occur within SELinux. One such example would be when a policy reload occurs. A **userspace object manager** could cache decision results and use the reload event as a trigger to flush their cache. The status file is read only by everyone and has no specific MAC permissions. The libselinux API interface is:

```
int selinux_status_open(int fallback);
void selinux_status_close();
int selinux_status_updated(void);
int selinux_status_getenforce(void);
int selinux_status_policyload(void);
int selinux_status_deny_unknown(void);
```

By checking the status structure, you can detect changes and flush the cache. Currently, however, you are missing this API in your libselinux, but we'll correct that in *Chapter 7, Utilizing Audit Logs*.

There are many SELinuxFS files in the file tree; our intent here was only to cover several files because of their importance or pertinence to what we've done and where we're going. We did not cover:

- `access`
- `checkreqprot`
- `commit_pending_bools`
- `context`
- `create`
- `deny_unknown`
- `member`
- `reject_unknown`
- `relabel`

The use of these files is not simple and is typically done by userspace object managers that are using the `libselinux` API to abstract the complexities.

Access Vector Cache

SELinuxFS also has some directories you can explore. The first is `avc`. This stands for "Access Vector Cache" and can be used to get statistics about the security server in the kernel:

```
root@udoo:/sys/fs/selinux # cd avc/
root@udoo:/sys/fs/selinux/avc # ls
cache_stats
cache_threshold
hash_stats
```

All these files can be read with the `cat` command:

```
root@udoo:/sys/fs/selinux/avc # cat cache_stats
lookups hits misses allocations reclaims frees
285710 285438 272 272 128 128
245827 245409 418 418 288 288
267511 267227 284 284 192 193
214328 213883 445 445 288 298
```

The `cache_stats` file is readable by all and requires no special MAC permissions.

The next file to look at is `hash_stats`:

```
root@udoo:/sys/fs/selinux/avc # cat hash_stats
entries: 512
buckets used: 284/512
longest chain: 7
```

The underlying data structure for the Access Vector Cache is a hash table; `hash_stats` lists the current properties. As we can see in the output of the preceding command, we have 512 slots in the table, with 284 of them in use. For collisions, we have the longest chain at 7 entries. This file is world readable and requires no special MAC permissions. You can modify the number of entries in this table through the `cache_threshold` file.

The `cache_threshold` file is used to tune the number of entries in the `avc` hash table. It is world readable and owner writeable. It requires the SELinux permission `setsecparam`, and can be written to and read from with the following simple commands, respectively:

```
root@udoo:/sys/fs/selinux/avc # echo "1024" > cache_threshold
root@udoo:/sys/fs/selinux/avc # echo 'cat cache_threshold'
1024
```

You can disable the cache by writing `0`. However, outside the benchmarking tests, this is not encouraged.

The booleans directory

The second directory to look into is `booleans`. An SELinux `boolean` allows policy statements to change dynamically via `boolean` conditions. By changing the `boolean` state, you can affect the behavior of the loaded policy. The current policy does not define any booleans; so this directory is empty. In policies that define booleans, the directory would be populated with files named after each boolean. You can then read and write to these files to change the `boolean` state. The Android toolbox has been modified to include the `getsebool` and `setsebool` commands. The `libselinux` API also exposes these capabilities:

```
int security_get_boolean_names(char ***names, int *len);
int security_get_boolean_pending(const char *name);
int security_get_boolean_active(const char *name);
```

```
int security_set_boolean(const char *name, int value);

int security_commit_booleans(void);

int security_set_boolean_list(size_t boolcnt, SELboolean * boollist, int
permanent);
```

Booleans are transactional. This means it is an all or nothing set. When you use
`security_set_boolean*`, you must call `security_commit_booleans()` to make it
take effect. Unlike Linux desktop systems, permanent booleans are not supported.
Changing the runtime value does not persist across reboots. Also, on Android, if
you are attempting Android **Compatibility Test Suite (CTS)** compliance, booleans
will cause the tests to fail. Booleans can have varying DAC permissions based on the
target, but they always require the SELinux permission, `setbool`.

 You must pass the Android Compatability Test Suite for Android
branding. More on CTS can be found at `https://source.`
`android.com/compatibility/cts-intro.html`.

The class directory

The next directory to look at is `class`. The `class` directory contains all the classes
defined in the `access_vectors` SELinux policy file or via the `class` keyword in the
SELinux policy language. For each class defined in the policy, a directory exists with
the same name. For instance, run the following on the serial terminal:

```
root@udoo:/sys/fs/selinux/class # ls -la

...

dr-xr-xr-x root root 1970-01-02 01:58 peer

dr-xr-xr-x root root 1970-01-02 01:58 process

dr-xr-xr-x root root 1970-01-02 01:58 property_service

dr-xr-xr-x root root 1970-01-02 01:58 rawip_socket

dr-xr-xr-x root root 1970-01-02 01:58 security

...
```

As you can see from the preceding command, there are quite a few directories.
Let's examine the `property_service` directory. This directory was chosen because it
is only one defined on Android. However, the files present in each directory are the
same and include `index` and `perms`:

```
root@udoo:/sys/fs/selinux/class/property_service # ls

index

perms
```

The mapping between string and some arbitrary integer that is defined in the SELinux kernel module is `index`. A directory that contains all the permissions possible for that class is `perms`:

```
root@udoo:/sys/fs/selinux/class/property_service # cd perms/
root@udoo:/sys/fs/selinux/class/property_service/perms # ls
set
```

As you can see, the `set` access vector is available for the `property_service` class. The `class` directory can be very beneficial to observe a policy file already loaded in a system.

The initial_contexts directory

The next directory entry to peer into is `initial_contexts`. This is the static mapping of the initial security contexts, better known as **security identifier (sid)**. This map tells the SELinux system which context should be used to start each kernel object:

```
root@udoo:/sys/fs/selinux/initial_contexts # ls
any_socket
devnull
file
...
```

We can see what the initial sid for `file` is by performing:

```
root@udoo:/sys/fs/selinux/initial_contexts # echo 'cat file'
u:object_r:unlabeled:s0
```

This corresponds to the entry in `external/sepolicy/initial_sid_contexts`:

```
...
sid file u:object_r:unlabeled:s0
...
```

The policy_capabilities directory

The last directory to look into is `policy_capabilities`. This directory defines any additional capabilities the policy might have. For our current setup, we should have:

```
root@udoo:/sys/fs/selinux/policy_capabilities # ls

network_peer_controls

open_perms
```

Each file entry contains a boolean indicating whether the feature is enabled:

```
root@udoo:/sys/fs/selinux/policy_capabilities # echo 'cat open_perms'

1
```

The entries are readable by all and writeable by none.

ProcFS

We alluded to some of the procfs interfaces that are being exported. Much of what is discussed is the security contexts, so that means the shell should have some security context associated with it... but how do we achieve this? Since this is a general mechanism that all LSMs use, the security contexts are both read and written through procfs:

```
root@udoo:/sys/fs/selinux/policy_capabilities # echo 'cat /proc/self/
attr/current'

u:r:init_shell:s0
```

You can also get per-thread contexts as well:

```
root@udoo:/sys/fs/selinux/policy_capabilities # echo '/proc/self/
task/2278/attr/current'

u:r:init_shell:s0
```

Just replace `2278` with the thread ID you want.

The DAC permissions on the current file are read and write for everyone, but those files are typically very restricted by MAC permissions. Typically, only the process that owns the procfs entry can read the files, and you must have both standard write permissions and a combination of `setcurrent`. Note that the "from" and "to" domains must be allowed using a **dyntransition**. To read, you must have `getattr`. All of these permissions are attained from the security class, `process`. The `libselinux` API functions `getcon` and `setcon` allow you to manipulate `current`.

The `prev` file can be used to find the previous context you switched from. This file is not writeable:

```
root@udoo:/proc/self/attr # echo 'cat prev'
u:r:init:s0
```

Our serial terminal's former domain or security context was `u:r:init:s0`.

The `exec` file is used to set the label for children processes. This is set before running an exec. All the permissions on these files are the same with respect to the MAC permissions used to actually set them. The caller attempting to set this must also hold `setexec` from the `process` class. The libselinux API `int setexeccon(security_context_t context)` and `int getexeccon(security_context_t *context)` can be used for setting and retrieving the label.

The `fscreate`, `keycreate`, and `sockcreate` files do similar things. When a process creates any one of the corresponding objects, `fs` objects (files, named pipes, or other objects), keys, or sockets, the values set here are used. The caller must also hold `setfscreate`, `setsockcreate`, and `setkeycreate` from the `process` class. The following SELinux API is used to alter these:

```
int set*createcon(security_context_t context);
int get*createcon(security_context_t *con);
```

Where `*` can be `fs`, `key`, or `socket`.

It's important to note that these special `process` class permissions give you the ability to change the `proc/attr` file. You still need to get through the DAC permissions and any SELinux permissions set on the file objects themselves. Then and only then do you need the additional permission, such as `setfscreate`.

Java SELinux API

Similar APIs to the C APIs discussed previously exist for Java as well. In this case, it is assumed you will build the code with the platform, as these are not public APIs shipped with the Android SDK. The API is located at `frameworks/base/core/java/android/os/SELinux.java`. However, this is a very limited subset of the API.

Summary

In this chapter, we explored the interface between the kernel and userspace with respect to SELinux, and reinforced the concepts of access vector class and security context. In the next chapter, we will perform some upgrades to our system and look at the audit logs getting one step closer to our ultimate goal — an operable device in SELinux enforcing mode. We say operable because we can put it in enforcing mode now. However, if you do it now via `setenforce 1` on a UDOO, your device will become unstable. On our system, for example, the browser fails to launch if we do this.

7
Utilizing Audit Logs

So far we've seen AVC records or the SELinux denial messages show up in dmesg, but dmesg is a circular memory buffer, subject to frequent rollover dependent on how verbose your kernel is. By using the audit kernel subsystem, we can route these messages into user space and log them to disk. On the desktop, the daemon that does this is called auditd. A minimal port of auditd is maintained in the NSA branches however, it has not officially been merged into AOSP. We are going to use the auditd version from the NSA branches since we are working on Android 4.3. The officially merged version as of April 7, 2014 can be found at https://android-review.googlesource.com/#/c/89645/. It's implemented within logd, and merged at https://android-review.googlesource.com/#/c/83526/.

In this chapter, we will:

- Update our system with the fast-paced SE for **Android Open Source Community (AOSP)**
- Investigate how the audit subsystem works
- Learn to read SELinux audit logs and start writing policy
- Look at contexts relative to the logs

All LSMs should log their messages into the audit subsystem. The audit subsystem can then route the messages to the kernel circular buffer using printk, or to the auditing daemon in user space, if one is present. The kernel and userspace logging daemon communicate using the AUDIT_NETLINK socket. We will dissect this interface further in the chapter.

Lastly, the audit subsystem has the capability to print comprehensive records when policy violations occur. Although you don't need this feature to enable and work with SELinux, it can make your life easier. To enable this system, you must use `auditd`, because `logd` currently doesn't have this support. You'll need to build your kernel with `CONFIG_AUDITSYSCALL=y` and place an `audit.rules` file in `/data/misc/audit/`. After you patch your tree with the following instructions, read `system/core/auditd/README`.

Unfortunately, the UDOO kernel version 3.0.35 does not support `CONFIG_AUDITSYSCALL`. The patch located at `https://git.kernel.org/cgit/linux/kernel/git/stable/linux-stable.git/commit/?id=29ef73b7a823b77a7cd0bdd7d7cded3fb6c2587b` should enable the support. However, on the UDOO, it causes a deadlock we could not trace down.

Upgrades – patches galore

Although Android 4.3, released from Google, had SE for Android support, it is still limited, especially in the areas of auditing. One of the simplest ways to bring this to a more useable state is to get the patches for some of the projects from the NSA's SE for Android 4.3 branch. Here, the community has staged and deployed many of the more advanced features which were not merged in the 4.3 timeframe.

The NSA maintains repositories at `https://bitbucket.org/seandroid/`. There are many projects so figuring out which to use and what branch can be daunting. A way to find them is to go through each project and find the projects with a `SEAndroid-4.3` branch. You don't need to descend into the device trees since we're not building AOSP devices. The list of such project is:

- `https://bitbucket.org/seandroid/system-core`
- `https://bitbucket.org/seandroid/frameworks-base`
- `https://bitbucket.org/seandroid/external-libselinux`
- `https://bitbucket.org/seandroid/build`
- `https://bitbucket.org/seandroid/frameworks-native`

We can also safely skip `sepolicy` since we've already updated it to the bleeding edge, but the kernels are a bit trickier. We need the changes from kernel-common (`https://bitbucket.org/seandroid/kernel-common`) and the binder patch (`https://android-review.googlesource.com/#/c/45984/`), which can be attained as follows:

```
$ mkdir ~/sepatches
$ cd ~/sepatches
```

```
$ git clone https://bitbucket.org/seandroid/system-core.git
$ git clone https://bitbucket.org/seandroid/frameworks-base.git
$ git clone https://bitbucket.org/seandroid/external-libselinux.git
$ git clone https://bitbucket.org/seandroid/build.git
$ git clone https://bitbucket.org/seandroid/frameworks-native.git
```

We can start by figuring out the exact version we need to patch to by looking at the `build/core/build_id.mk` file, and by using the webpage `https://source.android.com/source/build-numbers.html` to do a lookup.

The file shows `BUILD_ID` is `JSS15J`, and the lookup shows that we are working with the `android-4.3_r2.1` release for the UDOO.

For each downloaded project so far, generate the patches by running the command `git checkout origin/seandroid-4.3_r2`. Finally, execute `git format-patch origin/jb-mr2.0-release`. Since there is no `4.3._r2.1` branch, we're using `r2`.

For each of these patches, you'll need to apply them in the tree from their corresponding `udoo/<project>` folder. It is important to apply the patches for each project in numeric order starting with the `0001*` patch, moving on to `0002*`, and so on. As an example of how to apply a specific patch for a project, let's look at the first patch needed for `system-core`. Note that these Git repositories use hyphens in place of the slashes in the source tree; so `frameworks-base` correlates to `frameworks/base`.

First, generate the patches:

```
$ cd sepatches/system-core
$ git checkout origin/seandroid-4.3_r2
$ git format-patch origin/jb-mr2.0-release
```

Apply the first patch, as follows:

```
$ cd <udoo_root>/system/core
$ patch -p1 < ~/sepatches/system-core/0001-Add-writable-data-space-for-
radio.patch
patching file rootdir/init.rc
Reversed (or previously applied) patch detected! Assume -R? [n]
```

 Note that for UDOO, it is important not to apply a patch number higher than `0005` in `frameworks/base`. For other projects, you should apply all the patches.

Note the error. Just hit *Ctrl + C* to quit the patching process whenever you see this. The Git trees are not quite perfect, and because of this, some of the patches are already in the UDOO source. The patch command will let us know, and we can skip these by canceling them, when warned, with *Ctrl + C*. Keep going through the patches, canceling the ones already applied, and fixing up any failures. After patching userspace, it's *highly* recommended that you build to ensure nothing is broken.

Once userspace is completely patched, we need to patch the kernel. Start by cloning the kernel-common project from Bitbucket with the `git clone https://bitbucket.org/seandroid/kernel-common.git` command. We will patch the kernel with the same method as the rest of the projects with the exception of the binder patch. By viewing the link for the binder patch mentioned, `https://android-review.googlesource.com/#/c/45984/`, we found that the Git SHA hash is `a3c9991b560cf0a8dec1622fcc0edca5d0ced936`, as given in the **Patch set 4** reference field in the following screenshot:

We can then generate the patch for this SHA hash:

```
$ git format-patch -1 a3c9991b560cf0a8dec1622fcc0edca5d0ced936
0001-Add-security-hooks-to-binder-and-implement-the-hooks.patch
```

Then, apply that patch with the patch command as we did before. The patch has a failed hunk for a header file inclusion; just fix it up like the others by using the reject file. When you build, you'll get this error in the kernel:

```
security/selinux/hooks.c:1846:9: error: variable 'sad' has initializer
but incomplete type
security/selinux/hooks.c:1846:28: error: storage size of 'sad' isn't known
```

Go ahead and remove this line and all references. This was a change made in the 3.0 kernels:

```
struct selinux_audit_data sad = {0,};
ad.selinux_audit_data = &sad;
```

> We figured this out by looking through the original 3.0 patches, which can be found at following link:
>
> ```
> https://bitbucket.org/seandroid/kernel-omap/commits/
> 59bc19226c746f479edc2acca9a41f60669cbe82?at=seandro
> id-omap-tuna-3.0
> ```

As you recall, the UDOO uses a custom `init.rc`. We need to add any changes to `init.rc` to the one UDOO actually uses. All the patches that can modify `init.rc` will be in the system-core project, specifically these:

- `0003-Auditd-initial-commit.patch`
- `0007-Handle-policy-reloads-within-ueventd-rather-than-res.patch`
- `0009-Allow-system-UID-to-set-enforcing-and-booleans.patch`

Go ahead and find the changes to `init.rc` in these patches and apply them to `device/fsl/imx6/etc/init.rc` using the same patch technique.

The audit system

In the previous section, we did a lot of patching; the point of which was to enable the audit integration work done on Android and its dependencies. These patches also fix some bugs in the code and, very importantly, enable the SELinux/LSM binder hooks and policy controls.

The audit system in Linux is used by LSMs to print the denial records as well as to gather very thorough and complete records of events. No matter what, when an LSM prints a message, it gets propagated to the audit subsystem and printed. However, if the audit subsystem has been enabled, then you get more context associated with the denial. The audit subsystem even supports loading rules for watching this. For instance, you could watch all writes to /system that were not done by the system UID.

The auditd daemon

The auditd daemon, or service, runs in userspace and listens over a NETLINK socket to the audit subsystem. The daemon registers itself to receive the kernel messages, and can also load the audit rules over this socket. Once registered, the auditd daemon receives all the audit events. The auditd daemon was minimally ported, and there was an attempt to mainline it into Android that was later rejected. However, auditd has been used by various OEMs (such as Samsung) and by the NSA's 4.3 branch. An alternative approach that put records in logcat was later merged into Android (for more information, refer to https://android-review. googlesource.com/89645).

Earlier, we saw the AVC denial messages from SELinux in dmesg. The problem with this is that the circular memory log is prone to rollover when you have many denials or a chatty kernel. With auditd, all the messages come to the daemon and are written to the /data/misc/audit/audit.log file. This log file, herein referred to as audit. log, may exist on device boot and is rotated into the /data/misc/audit/audit.old file, known as audit.old. The daemon resumes logging to a new audit.log file. This rotate event occurs when the size threshold AUDITD_MAX_LOG_FILE_SIZEKB (set during compile time in the system/core/auditd/Android.mk file) is exceeded. This threshold is typically 1000 KB but can be changed in the device's makefile. Also, sending SIGHUP with kill will cause a rotate as in the following example.

Verify the daemon is running and get its PID:

```
root@udoo:/ # ps -Z | grep audit
u:r:auditd:s0 audit 2281 1 /system/bin/auditd
u:r:kernel:s0 root 2293 2 kauditd
```

Verify only one log exists:

```
root@udoo:/ # ls -la /data/misc/audit/
-rw-r----- audit system 79173 1970-01-02 00:19 audit.log
```

Rotate the logs:

```
root@udoo:/ # kill -SIGHUP 2281
```

Verify `audit.old`:

```
root@udoo:/ # ls -la /data/misc/audit/
-rw-r----- audit system 319 1970-01-02 00:20 audit.log
-rw-r----- audit system 79173 1970-01-02 00:19 audit.old
```

Auditd internals

Since the `auditd` and `libaudit` code from the Linux desktop have a GPL license, a rewrite was done for Android, released under the Apache license. The rewrite is minimal, thus you will only find the functions implemented that were required to support the daemon. The functional and header interfaces should remain identical though.

The `auditd` daemon starts life at `main()` in `system/core/auditd.c`. It quickly changes its permissions from UID root to a special `auditd` UID. When it does this, it retains `CAPSYS_AUDIT`, which is a required DAC capability check to use the `AUDIT NETLINK` socket. It does this via a call to `drop_privileges_or_die()`. From there, it does some option parsing with `getopt()`, and we finally get to the audit-specific calls, the first of which opens the NETLINK socket using `audit_open()`. This function simply calls `socket(PF_NETLINK, SOCK_RAW, NETLINK_AUDIT)`, which opens a file descriptor to the NETLINK socket. After opening the socket, the daemon opens a handle to `audit.log` with a call to `audit_log_open(const char *logfile, const char *rotatefile, size_t threshold)`. This function checks whether the `audit.log` file exists and, if it does, renames it to `audit.old`. It then creates a new empty log file in which the data is recorded.

The next step is to register the daemon with the audit subsystem so that it knows to whom to send messages. By setting the PID of the daemon, you ensure that only this daemon will get the messages. Since NETLINK can support many readers, you don't want a "rogue auditd" to read the messages. With that stated, the daemon calls `audit_set_pid(audit_fd, getpid(), WAIT_YES)`, where `audit_fd` is the NETLINK socket from `audit_open()`, `getpid()` returns the daemon's PID, and `WAIT_YES` causes the daemon to block until the operation is complete. Next, the daemon enables the audit subsystem's advanced features with a call to `audit_set_enabled(audit_fd, 1)` and adds rules to the audit subsystem via `audit_rules_read_and_add(audit_fd, AUDITD_RULES_FILE)`. This function reads the rules from that file, formats some structures, and sends those structures to the kernel.

The `audit_set_enabled()` and `audit_rules_read_and_add()` only have an effect if the kernel is built with `CONFIG_AUDITSYSCALL`. After this, the daemon checks whether the `-k` option was specified. The `-k` option tells `auditd` to look in `dmesg` for any missed audit records. It does this because there is a race between capturing audit records before the circular buffer overflows and userspace starting many services, generating audit events and policy violations. Essentially, this helps coalesce the audit events from early boot into the same log files.

After this, the daemon enters a loop to read from the NETLINK socket, formatting the messages, and writing them to the log file. It starts this loop by waiting for IO on the NETLINK socket using `poll()`. If `poll()` exits with an error, the loop continues to check the `quit` variable. If `EINTR` is raised, the loop guard, `quit`, is set to `true` in the signal handler, and the daemon exits. If `poll()` is data on the NETLINK, the daemon calls `audit_get_reply(audit_fd, &rep, GET_REPLY_BLOCKING, 0)`, getting an `audit_reply` structure back with the `rep` parameter. It then writes the `audit_reply` structure (with formatting) to the `audit.log` file with `audit_log_write(alog, "type=%d msg=%.*s\n", rep.type, rep.len, rep.msg.data)`. It does this until `EINTR` is raised, at which point, the daemon exits.

When the daemon exits, it clears the PID registered with the kernel (`audit_set_pid(audit_fd, 0)`), closes the audit socket via `audit_close()` (which is really just the syscall, `close(audit_fd)`), and closes the `audit.log` with `audit_log_close()`. The `audit_log_*` family of functions is not part of the GPLed interface to audit and is a custom write.

When Google ported `auditd` to the `logd` infrastructure in Android, it used the same functions and library code used by the daemon's `main()` and wrapped it into `logd`. However, Google *did not* take the `audit_set_enabled()` and `audit_rules_read_and_add()` functions.

Interpreting SELinux denial logs

The SELinux denials get routed to the kernel audit subsystem, to `auditd`, and finally, to `audit.log` and `audit.old`. With the logs resident in `audit.log`, let's pull this file over `adb` and have a closer look at it.

Run the following command from the host, with `adb` enabled:

```
$ adb pull /data/misc/audit/audit.log
```

Now, let's tail that file and look for these lines:

```
$ tail audit.log

...

type=1400 msg=audit(88526.980:312): avc: denied { getattr } for pid=3083
comm="adbd" path="/data/misc/audit/audit.log" dev=mmcblk0p4 ino=42
scontext=u:r:adbd:s0 tcontext=u:object_r:audit_log:s0 tclass=file

type=1400 msg=audit(88527.030:313): avc: denied { read } for pid=3083
comm="adbd" name="audit.log" dev=mmcblk0p4 ino=42 scontext=u:r:adbd:s0
tcontext=u:object_r:audit_log:s0 tclass=file

type=1400 msg=audit(88527.030:314): avc: denied { open } for pid=3083
comm="adbd" name="audit.log" dev=mmcblk0p4 ino=42 scontext=u:r:adbd:s0
tcontext=u:object_r:audit_log:s0 tclass=file
```

The records here consist of two major portions: `type` and `msg`. The `type` field indicates what type of message it is. Messages with type 1400 are AVC messages, which are SELinux denial messages (there are other types, as well). The `msg` (short for message) portion of the preceding policy contains the part for us to analyze.

The last command we executed was `adb pull /data/misc/audit/aduit.log` and, as you can see, we have a few `adb` policy violations at the tail of the `audit.log` file. Let's start by looking at this event:

```
type=1400 msg=audit(88526.980:312): avc: denied { getattr } for pid=3083
comm="adbd" path="/data/misc/audit/audit.log" dev=mmcblk0p4 ino=42
scontext=u:r:adbd:s0 tcontext=u:object_r:audit_log:s0 tclass=file
```

We can see that the `comm` field is `adbd`. However, it's not wise to trust this value since it can be controlled from userspace using the `prctl()` interface. It can only be viewed as a hint. The best way to verify this is to check the PID using `ps -Z`:

```
# ps -Z | grep adbd
u:r:adbd:s0 root 3083 1 /sbin/adbd
```

With the daemon verified, we can now check the message in more detail. The message consists of the following fields (optional fields are identified by `*`):

- `avc: denied`: This part will always happen and denotes it is a denial record.
- `{ permission }`: This is the permission that was denied, in this case, `getattr`.
- `for`: This will always be printed and makes the output readable.
- `Path*`: This is the optional field that contains the path of the object in question. It only makes sense for filesystem access denials.
- `dev*`: This is the optional field that identifies the block device for the mounted filesystem. It only makes sense for filesystem access denials.
- `ino*`: This is the optional inode of the file. Only the anonymous files in Linux print inode. It only makes sense for filesystem access denials.
- `tclass`: This is the target class of the object, which in our case was `file`.

At this point, we need to understand what the `msg` portion of the denial record is telling us at a very distilled level. It is saying that the Android debug bridge daemon wants to be able to call `getattr` on our policy file. A few events down, we will see it also wants `read` and `open`. This is the side effect of running `adb pull`. A `getattr` permission denial occurs from a `stat()` syscall, and the `read/open` are from `read()` and `open()` syscalls. If you want to allow this in your policy, which would be a security decision based on your threat model, you should add:

```
allow adbd audit_log:file { getattr read open };
```

Alternatively, use the macro sets defined in `global_macros`:

```
allow adbd audit_log:file r_file_perms;
```

Most of the time, you should use the macros defined in `global_macros` for file permission accesses. Typically, adding them one by one is very time consuming and tedious. The macros group the permissions in a context analogous to read, write, and execute DAC permissions. For instance, if you give it `open` and `read`, there's a good chance at some point that the source domain will need to stat the file. So, the `r_file_perms` macro has those permissions in it already.

You should add this rule to `external/sepolicy/adbd.te`. The `.te` files (also called `type enforcement` files) are organized by source context, so make sure you add it to the correct file. We do not recommend adding this allow rule—there's no legitimate reason that `adbd` needs access to the audit logs—we can safely ignore these with a `dontaudit` rule:

```
dontaudit adbd audit_log:file r_file_perms;
```

The `dontaudit` rule is a policy statement that says don't audit (print) denials that match this rule.

If you're not sure what to do, the best advice is to leverage the mailing lists for SE for Android, SELinux, and audit. Just keep the messages appropriate to the specific mailing lists topic.

A tool exists called `audit2allow`, which can help you write policy allow rules. However, it's only a tool and can be misused. It translates the policy file to the allow rules for the policy:

```
$ cat audit.log | audit2allow
#============= adbd ==============
allow adbd audit_log:file { read getattr open };
```

The `audit2allow` tool is not macro aware or aware if you really want to add this allow rule to the policy file. Only the policy author can make this decision.

There is also a tool to enable the `r_file_*` macro mapping called `fixup.py`. You can get the tool at `https://bitbucket.org/billcroberts/fixup/overview`. After downloading, make it executable, and place it somewhere in your executable path:

```
$ chmod a+x fixup.py
$ cat audit.log | audit2allow | fixup.py
#============= adbd ==============
allow adbd audit_log:file r_file_perms;
```

Contexts

In the simplest sense, writing policies is just the activity of identifying policy violations and adding the appropriate allow rules to the policy file. However, in order for SELinux to be effective, the source and target contexts must be correct. If they are not, the allow rules are meaningless.

The first things you might encounter are denials where the target type is unlabeled. In this case, the proper target label needs to be set (refer to *Chapter 11, Labeling Properties*). Also, process labels can be wrong. Multiple processes can belong to a domain, and unless explicitly done via policy, the child process of a parent inherits the parent's domain. However, in Android, domains that have multiple processes are quite limited. You will never see multiple processes in init, system_server, adbd, auditd, debuggerd, dhcp, servicemanager, vold, netd, surfaceflinger, drmserver, mediaserver, installd, keystore, sdcardd, wpa, and zygote domains.

It's okay to see multiple processes in the following domains:

* system_app
* untrusted_app
* platform_app
* shared_app
* media_app
* release_app
* isolated_app
* shell

On a released device, nothing should be run in the su, recovery, and init_shell domains. The following table provides a complete mapping of domains to the expected executables and cardinality:

Domain	Executable(s)	Cardinality (N)
u:r:init:s0"	/init	N == 1
u:r:ueventd:s0	/sbin/ueventd	N == 1
u:r:healthd:s0	/sbin/healthd	N == 1
u:r:servicemanager:s0	/system/bin/servicemanager	N == 1
u:r:vold:s0	/system/bin/vold	N == 1
u:r:netd:s0	/system/bin/netd	N == 1
u:r:debuggerd:s0	/system/bin/debuggerd, /system/bin/debuggerd64	N == 1
u:r:surfaceflinger:s0	/system/bin/surfaceflinger	N == 1
u:r:zygote:s0	zygote, zygote64	N == 1
u:r:drmserver:s0	/system/bin/drmserver	N == 1
u:r:mediaserver:s0	/system/bin/mediaserver	N >= 1

Domain	Executable(s)	Cardinality (N)
u:r:installd:s0	/system/bin/installd	N == 1
u:r:keystore:s0	/system/bin/keystore	N == 1
u:r:system_server:s0	system_server	N ==1
u:r:sdcardd:s0	/system/bin/sdcard	N >=1
u:r:watchdogd:s0	/sbin/watchdogd	N >=0 && N < 2
u:r:wpa:s0	/system/bin/wpa_supplicant	N >=0 && N < 2
u:r:init_shell:s0	null	N == 0
u:r:recovery:s0	null	N == 0
u:r:su:s0	null	N == 0

Several **Compatibility Test Suite (CTS)** tests have been written around this and submitted to AOSP at `https://android-review.googlesource.com/#/c/82861/`.

Based on these generic assertions of what a good policy should look like, let's evaluate ours.

First, we will check for unlabeled objects. From the host, with the `audit.log` file you obtained with `adb pull`:

```
$ cat audit.log | grep unlabeled
...
type=1400 msg=audit(86527.670:341): avc: denied { rename } for pid=3206
comm="pool-1-thread-1" name="com.android.settings_preferences.xml"
dev=mmcblk0p4 ino=129664 scontext=u:r:system_app:s0 tcontext=u:object_r:u
nlabeled:s0 tclass=file
...
```

It looks like we have some files and other things that are not labeled properly; we will address these in the *Chapter 11, Labeling Properties*. Now, let's check for domains that have multiple processes when they should not, and find improper binaries in those domains (refer to the previous table for the complete mapping.)

Init:

```
$ adb shell ps -Z | grep u:r:init:s0
u:r:init:s0 root 1 0 /init
u:r:init:s0 root 2267 1 /sbin/watchdogd
```

Zygote:

```
$ adb shell ps -Z | grep u:r:zygote:s0
u:r:zygote:s0 root 2285 1 zygote
$ adb shell ps -Z | grep u:r:init_shell
u:r:init_shell:s0 root 2278 1 /system/bin/sh
... through all domains
```

After doing this, we found issues because something is running in the init_shell domain, and watchdogd is in the init domain. These must be corrected.

Summary

Writing sepolicy is relatively easy, writing good policy is an art. It requires the policy author to understand the system and the implications of the allow rule. Policy itself is a meta-programming language where the language controls how userspace and the kernel get along, and much like any program, the policy can be architected for a specific use. Policies can be too porous (essentially useless) or very tight and difficult to change without breaking the portions that already work.

A good policy needs to preserve the intended proper function of the system, so thorough testing of all the systems within Android is essential. CTS is a great help in exercising Android, but it often does not cover all the cases; user testing is recommended. In the next chapter, we will cover how filesystems and filesystem objects get their security labels and how we can change them. Later, we will go over how to use CTS as a tool to test the system and generate policy violations for intended behaviors.

8
Applying Contexts to Files

In the last chapter, we upgraded our system, collected the audit logs, and started to analyze the audit records. We discovered that some objects on the filesystem were unlabeled. In this chapter, we will:

- Learn how filesystems and filesystem objects get their labels
- Demonstrate techniques to change labels
- Introduce extended attributes for labeling
- Investigate file contexts and dynamic type transitions

Labeling filesystems

Filesystems on Linux originate from mount, with the exception of `ramdisk rootfs` on Android. Filesystems on Linux vary drastically. In general, in order to support all the features of SELinux, you need a filesystem with the support for `xattr` and the `security` namespace. We saw this requirement when we were setting up the kernel configuration.

Filesystem objects, as they are created, all start with an initial context, just like all other kernel objects. Contexts on files simply inherit from their parent, so if the parent is unlabeled, then the child is unlabeled, with the exception of a type transition rule. Typically, if the context is unlabeled, it infers that the data was created on a filesystem prior to enabling SELinux support, or the type label in the `xattr` does not exist in the currently loaded policy.

The initial label or initial **security id (sid)**, is in the `sepolicy` file `initial_sid_` `contexts`. Each object class has its associated initial `sid` present. For example, let's take a look at the following code snippet:

```
. . .
sid fs u:object_r:labeledfs:s0
sid file u:object_r:unlabeled:s0
. . .
```

fs_use

Filesystems can be labeled in a variety of ways. The best case scenario is when the filesystem supports `xattrs`. In that case, an `fs_use_xattr` statement should appear in the policy. These statements appear in the `fs_use` file in the `sepolicy` directory. The syntax for `fs_use_xattr` is:

fs_use_xattr <fstype> <context>

To look at `fs_use` from `sepolicy`, we can refer to an example for the `ext4` filesystems:

```
. . .
fs_use_xattr ext3 u:object_r:labeledfs:s0;
fs_use_xattr ext4 u:object_r:labeledfs:s0;
fs_use_xattr xfs u:object_r:labeledfs:s0;
. . .
```

This tells SELinux that when it encounters an `ext4` `fs` object; look in the extended attributes for the label or file context.

fs_task_use

The other way a filesystem can be labeled is by using the process' context while creating objects. This makes sense for pseudo filesystems where the objects are really process contexts, such as `pipefs` and `sockfs`. These pseudo filesystems manage the pipe and socket syscalls and are not really mounted to userspace. They exist internally to the kernel, for the kernels use. However, they do have objects, and like any other object, they need to be labeled. This is the context in which the `fs_task_` `use` policy statement makes sense. These internal filesystems can only be accessed by processes directly, and provide services to those processes. Hence, labeling them with the creator makes sense. The syntax is as follows:

fs_task_use <fstype> <context>

Examples from the `sepolicy` file `fs_use` are as follows:

```
...
# Label inodes from task label.
fs_use_task pipefs u:object_r:pipefs:s0;
fs_use_task sockfs u:object_r:sockfs:s0;
...
```

fs_use_trans

The next way you might wish to set labels on pseudo filesystems that are actually mounted, is by using `fs_use_trans`. This sets a filesystem wide label on the pseudo filesystem. The syntax for this is as follows:

fs_use_trans <fstype> <context>

Example from the `sepolicy` file `fs_use` is as follows:

```
...
fs_use_trans devpts u:object_r:devpts:s0;
fs_use_trans tmpfs u:object_r:tmpfs:s0;
...
```

genfscon

If none of the `fs_use_*` statements meet your use cases, which would be the case for `vfat` filesystems and `procfs`, then you would use the `genfscon` statement. The label specified for `genfscon` applies to *all* instances of that filesystem mount. For instance, you might wish to use `genfscon` with the `vfat` filesystems. If you have two `vfat` mounts, they will use the same `genfscon` statement for each mount. However, `genfscon` behaves differently with `procfs`, and lets you label each file or directory within the filesystem.

The syntax of `genfscon` is as follows:

genfscon <fstype> <path> <context>

Examples from `sepolicy` `genfs_contexts` are as follows:

```
...
# Label inodes with the fs label.
genfscon rootfs / u:object_r:rootfs:s0
# proc labeling can be further refined (longest matching prefix).
genfscon proc / u:object_r:proc:s0
genfscon proc /net/xt_qtaguid/ctrl u:object_r:qtaguid_proc:s0
...
```

Note that the `rootfs` partial path is `/`. It's not `procfs`, so it doesn't support any fine granularity to its labeling; so `/` is the only thing you can use. However, you can get wild with `procfs` and set to any granularity you desire.

Mount options

Another option, if none of those fit your needs, is to pass the `context` option via the `mount` command line. This sets a filesystem wide mount context, such as `genfscon`, but is useful in the case of multiple filesystems that need to have separate labels. For instance, if you have two `vfat` filesystems mounted, you might wish to separate accesses to them. With `genfscon` statements, both filesystems would use the same label provided by `genfscon`. By specifying the label at mount time, you can have two `vfat` filesystems mounted with different labels.

Take the following command as an example:

```
mount -ocontext=u:object_r:vfat1:s0 /dev/block1 /mnt/vfat1
mount -ocontext=u:object_r:vfat2:s0 /dev/block1 /mnt/vfat2
```

Additional to the context as a mount option are: `fscontext` and `defcontext`. These options are mutually exclusive from context. The `fscontext` option sets the meta filesystem type that is used for certain operations, such as mount, but does not change the per file labels. The `defcontext` sets the default context for unlabeled files overriding the `initial_sid` statements. Lastly, another option, `rootcontext` allows you to set the root inode context in the filesystem, but only for that object. According to the man page mount (`man 8 mount`), it was found useful in stateless Linux.

Labeling with extended attributes

Lastly, and probably the most frequently used way of labeling, is by using the extended attributes support also known as `xattr` or EA support. Even with `xattr` support, new objects inherit the context of their parent directory; however, these labels have the granularity of being per filesystem object-based or inode-based. If you remember, we had to turn on or verify that XATTR(CONFIG_EXT4_FS_XATTR) support was enabled for our filesystems on Android as well as configuring SELinux to use it via the config option CONFIG_EXT4_FS_SECURITY.

Extended attributes are a key-value metadata stores for files. SELinux security contexts use the `security.selinux` key, and the value is a string that is the security context or label.

The file_contexts file

Within the `sepolicy` directory, you will find the `file_contexts` file. This file is consulted to set the attributes on filesystems that support per file security labels. Note that a couple of pseudo filesystems support this as well, such as `tmpfs`, `sysfs`, and recently `rootfs`. The `file_context` file has a regular expression-based syntax as follows, where `regexp` is the regular expression for the path:

```
regexp <type> ( <file label> | <<none>> )
```

If multiple regular expressions are defined for a file, the last match is used, so order is important.

The following list shows each type field value for the type of filesystem object, their meanings, and syscall interface:

- `--`: This denotes a regular file.
- `-d`: This denotes a directory.
- `-b`: This denotes a block file.
- `-s`: This denotes a socket file.
- `-c`: This denotes a character file.
- `-l`: This denotes a link file.
- `-p`: This denotes a named pipe file.

As you can see, the type is essentially the mode as output by `ls -la` command. If it's not specified, it matches everything.

The next field is the file label or the special identifier `<<none>>`. Either one would supply a context or the identifier `<<none>>`. If you specify the context, the SELinux tools that consult `file_contexts` use the last match to the specified context. If the context specified is `<<none>>`, it means that no context is assigned. So, leave the one that we have found. The keyword `<<none>>` is not used in the AOSP reference, `sepolicy`.

It's important to note that the preceding paragraph explicitly states that SELinux tools use the `file_contexts` policy. The kernel is not aware that this file exists. SELinux labels all its objects by explicitly setting them from userspace with tools that look up the context in `file_context` or via the `fs_use_*` and `genfs` policy statements. In other words, `file_contexts` is not built in the core policy file, and it is not loaded or used directly by the kernel. At build time, the `file_contexts` file is built in the ramdisk rootfs and can be found at `/file_contexts`. Also, during build time, the system image is labeled, freeing the device itself from this burden.

In Android, `init`, `ueventd`, and `installd` have all been modified to look up the contexts of objects they are creating; so that they can label them properly. Thus, all the init built ins that create filesystem objects, such as `mkdir`, have been modified to make use of the `file_contexts` file if it exists, and the same goes for `installd` and `ueventd`.

Let's take a look at some snippets from the `file_context` file located in `sepolicy`:

```
...
/dev(/.*)? u:object_r:device:s0
/dev/accelerometer u:object_r:sensors_device:s0
/dev/alarm u:object_r:alarm_device:s0
...
```

Here, we are setting up the contexts for files in `/dev`. Note how the entries are in order from most generic to more specific `dev` files. Thus, any files not covered by the more specific entries will end up with the context `u:object_r:device:s0`, and the files that match further down, end up with a more specific label. For instance, the accelerometer at `/dev/accelerometer` will get the context `u:object_r:sensors_device:s0`. Note that the type field was omitted, which means that it matches on *all* filesystem objects, such as directories (`type -d`).

You might be wondering how `/dev`, the directory itself, gets a file context. Looking at some of the snippets, we say the / or root, got labeled via the statement `genfscon rootfs / u:object_r:rootfs:s0` in the `genfs_context` file. This chapter stated earlier that, "new objects inherit the context of their parent directory." Hence, we can reason that `/dev` is of context `u:object_r:rootfs:s0` since that is the label / has. We can test this by passing the `-Z` flag to `ls` to show us the label of `/dev`. On the UDOO serial connection, execute the following command:

```
130|root@udoo:/ # ls -laZ /
...
drwxr-xr-x root root u:object_r:device:s0 dev
...
```

It seems that the hypothesis is incorrect, but note that it is true that everything has a label, and if it's not specified, then it inherits from the parent. Looking back at `sepolicy`, we can see that the `dev` filesystem was initially set with a `fs_use_trans devtmpfs u:object_r:device:s0;` policy statement. So when the filesystem is mounted, it is set filesystem wide. Later, when entries are added by `init` or `ueventd`, they use `file_contexts` entries to set the context of the newly created filesystem object to what is specified in the `file_contexts` file. The filesystem at `/dev`, which is a `devtmps` pseudo filesystem, is an example of a filesystem that has both a filesystem-wide label via the `fs_use_trans` statement, but can also support fine grained labeling via `file_contexts;`. Filesystems are not very consistent in capabilities on Linux.

Dynamic type transitions

Dynamic type transitions indicated by the SELinux policy statement `type_transition` are a way to allow files to dynamically determine their types. Because these are compiled into the policy, these do not have any relation to the `file_contexts` file. These policy statements allow the policy author to dynamically dictate the context of a file based on the context in which the file is created. These are useful in situations where you don't control source code, or do not wish to couple SELinux in any way. For instance, the `wpa` supplicant, which is a service that runs for Wi-Fi support and creates a socket file in its data directory. Its data directory is labeled with the type `wifi_data_file` and as expected, the socket ends up with that label. However, this socket is shared by the system server. Now, we can allow just the system server to access the type and object class, however, `hostapd` and other things are creating sockets and other objects in that directory and thus the objects also have this type. We really want to ensure that the two sockets in question, the one used by `hostapd` and the other by system server, are kept exclusive from each other. To do this, we need to be able to label one of the sockets at a finer granularity, and to do so, we can either modify the code or use a dynamic type transition. Rather than mucking with the code, let's use a type transition, as follows:

```
type_transition wpa wifi_data_file:sock_file wpa_socket;
```

This is an actual statement from the `sepolicy` file, `wpa_supplicant.te`. It says that, when a process of the type `wpa` creates a file of the type `wifi_data_file` and the object class is `sock_file` to label it as `wpa_socket` on creation. The statement syntax is as follows:

```
type_transition <creating type> <created type>:<class> <new type>;
```

As of SELinux policy version 25, the `type_transition` statement can support named type transitions where a fourth argument exists and is the name of the file:

```
type_transition <creating type> <created type>:<class> <new type>
<file name>;
```

We will see an example use of this filename in the `sepolicy` file, `system_server.te`:

```
type_transition system_server system_data_file:sock_file system_
ndebug_socket "ndebugsocket";
```

Note the filename or basename and not the path, and it must match exactly. Regex is not supported. It's also interesting to note that the dynamic transitions are not limited to file objects, but any object class event processes. We will see how dynamic process transitions are used in *Chapter 9, Adding Services to Domains*.

Examples and tools

With the theory behind us, let's look at the tools and techniques to label files in the system. Let's start by mounting a `ramfs` filesystem. We will start by remounting / since it is read only and create a mount point for the filesystem. Via the UDOO serial console, execute:

```
root@udoo:/ # mount -oremount,rw /
root@udoo:/ # mkdir /ramdisk
root@udoo:/ # mount -t ramfs -o size=20m ramfs /ramdisk
```

Now, we want to see which label the filesystem has:

```
# ls -laZ / | grep ramdisk
drwxr-xr-x root root u:object_r:unlabeled:s0 ramdisk
```

As you can recall, the `initial_sid_context` file had this initial `sid` set for the filesystem:

```
sid file u:object_r:unlabeled:s0
```

If we want to get this ramdisk in a new label, we need to create the type in the policy, and set a new `genfscon` statement to use it. We will declare the new type in the sepolicy file `file.te`:

```
type ramdisk, file_type, fs_type;
```

The type policy statement syntax is as follows:

```
type <new type>, <attribute0,attribute1...attributeN>;
```

Attributes in SELinux are statements that let you define common groups. They are defined via the `attribute` statement. In Android SELinux policy, we have `file_type` and `fs_type` defined for us already. We will use them here because this new type, which we're creating, has the attributes `file_type` and `fs_type`. The `file_type` attribute is associated with a type for a file, and the `fs_type` attribute means that this type is also associated with filesystems. Attributes, right now, are not of great importance; so don't get caught up in the detail.

The next thing to modify is the `sepolicy` file, `genfs_context` by adding the following:

```
genfscon ramfs / u:object_r:ramdisk:s0
```

Now, we will compile the boot image and flash it to the device, or better yet, let's use the dynamic policy reload support like the following.

From the root of the UDOO project tree build just the `sepolicy` project:

```
$ mmm external/sepolicy/
```

Push the new policy over `adb`, as follows:

```
$ adb push $OUT/root/sepolicy /data/security/current/sepolicy
544 KB/s (86409 bytes in 0.154s)
```

Trigger a reload by using the `setprop` command:

```
$ adb shell setprop selinux.reload_policy 1
```

If you have the serial console connected, you should see:

```
SELinux: Loaded policy from /data/security/current/sepolicy
```

If you don't, and just have `adb`, check `dmesg`:

```
$ adb shell dmesg | grep "SELinux: Loaded"
<4>SELinux: Loaded policy from /sepolicy
<6>init: SELinux: Loaded property contexts from /property_contexts
<4>SELinux: Loaded policy from /data/security/current/sepolicy
```

A successful load should use our policy at the path, `/data/security/current/sepolicy`. Let's unmount the ramdisk and remount it to check out its type:

```
root@udoo:/ # umount /ramdisk
root@udoo:/ # mount -t ramfs -o size=20m ramfs /ramdisk
root@udoo:/ # ls -laZ / | grep ramdisk
drwxr-xr-x root root u:object_r:ramdisk:s0 ramdisk
```

We were able to modify the policy and use `genfscon` to change the filesystem type, and now to show inheritance, let's go ahead and create a file on the filesystem with `touch`:

```
root@udoo:/ # cd /ramdisk
root@udoo:/ramdisk # touch hello
root@udoo:/ramdisk # ls -Z
-rw------- root root u:object_r:ramdisk:s0 hello
```

As we expected, the new file is labeled with the type ramdisk. Now, suppose when we do touch from the shell, we want the file to be of a different type, such as ramdisk_ newfile; how can we do this? We can do this by modifying touch itself to consult file_contexts, or we can define a dynamic type transition; let us try the dynamic type transition approach. The first argument to the type_transition statement is the creating type; so what type is our shell in? You can get this by performing:

```
root@udoo:/ramdisk # echo `cat /proc/self/attr/current`
u:r:init_shell:s0
```

A simpler way is to run the id -Z command, which uses the aforementioned proc file. For a serial console, execute:

```
root@udoo:/ramdisk # id -Z
uid=0(root) gid=0(root) context=u:r:init_shell:s0
```

And to run the same command for the adb shell:

```
$ adb shell id -Z
uid=0(root) gid=0(root) context=u:r:shell:s0
```

Note the discrepancy between our serial console shell and the adb shell, in *Chapter 9, Adding Services to Domains*; we will fix this. Because of this, the policy we author now will address both cases.

Start by opening the sepolicy file, init_shell.te and append the following to the end of the file:

```
type_transition init_shell ramdisk:file ramdisk_newfile;
```

Do this for the sepolicy file, shell.te:

```
type_transition shell ramdisk:file ramdisk_newfile;
```

Now, we need to declare the new type; so open up the sepolicy file, file.te and append the following:

```
type ramdisk_newfile, file_type;
```

Note that we have only used the file_type attribute. This is because a filesystem should never have the type ramdisk_newfile, only a file residing within that file system should.

Now, build the `adb` policy, push it to the device, and trigger a reload. With that done, create the file and check the results:

```
$ adb shell 'touch /ramdisk/shell_newfile'
$ adb shell 'ls -laZ /ramdisk'
-rw-rw-rw- root root u:object_r:ramdisk:s0 shell_newfile
```

So it didn't work. Let's investigate the reason by trying on an example of an `ext4` filesystem. Let's use the following commands:

```
root@udoo:/ # cd /data/
root@udoo:/data # mkdir ramdisk
```

Now, check its context:

```
root@udoo:/data # ls -laZ | grep ramdisk
drwx------ root rootu:object_r:system_data_file:s0 ramdisk
```

The label is `system_data_file`. This is not helpful, as it doesn't apply to our type transition rule; to fix this, we can use the `chcon` command to explicitly change the files context:

```
root@udoo:/data # chcon u:object_r:ramdisk:s0 ramdisk
root@udoo:/data # ls -laZ | grep ramdisk
drwx------ root root u:object_r:ramdisk:s0 ramdisk
```

Now with the context changed to match what we were trying earlier with the ramdisk, let's try to create a file within this directory:

```
root@udoo:/data/ramdisk # touch newfile
root@udoo:/data/ramdisk # ls -laZ
-rw------- root root u:object_r:ramdisk_newfile:s0 newfile
```

As you can see, the type transition has occurred. This was meant to illustrate the issues you may find while working with SELinux and Android. Now that we have shown that our `type_transition` statement is valid, there are only two possibilities why this is failing: the filesystem doesn't support it or we're missing something somewhere to "turn it on". It turns out that the latter is the case; we were missing our `fs_use_trans` statements. So go ahead and open up the `sepolicy` file, `fs_use` and add the following line:

```
    fs_use_trans ramfs u:object_r:ramdisk:s0;
```

This statement enables SELinux dynamic transitions on this filesystem. Now, rebuild the `sepolicy` project, `adb push` the policy file, and enable a dynamic reload via `setprop`:

```
$ mmm external/sepolicy
$ adb push $OUT/root/sepolicy /data/security/current/sepolicy546 KB/s
(86748 bytes in 0.154s)
$ adb shell setprop selinux.reload_policy 1
root@udoo:/ # cd ramdisk
root@udoo:/ramdisk # touch foo
root@udoo:/ramdisk # ls -Z
-rw------- root root u:object_r:ramdisk_newfile:s0 foo
```

There you have it, the object has the right value determined by a dynamic type transition. We were missing `fs_use_trans`, which enabled type transitions on filesystems that don't support `xattrs`.

Now, suppose we want to mount another ramdisk, what would happen? Well since it was labeled with the `genfscon` statement, all filesystems mounted with that type should get the context, `u:object_r:ramdisk:s0`. We will mount this filesystem at `/ramdisk2`, and verify this behavior:

```
root@udoo:/ # mkdir ramdisk2
root@udoo:/ # mount -t ramfs -o size=20m ramfs /ramdisk2
```

Also, check the contexts:

```
root@udoo:/ # ls -laZ | grep ramdisk
drwxr-xr-x root root u:object_r:ramdisk:s0 ramdisk
drwxr-xr-x root root u:object_r:ramdisk:s0 ramdisk2
```

If we want to write allow rules to separate accesses to these file systems, we will need to have their target files in separate types. To do this, we can mount the new ramdisk with the context option. But first, we need to create the new type; lets go to the `sepolicy` file, `file.te` and add a new type called `ramdisk2`:

```
type ramdisk2, file_type, fs_type;
```

Now, build the `sepolicy` with the command `mmm`, followed be using the command `abd push` to push the policy, and trigger a reload with the `setprop` command:

```
$ mmm external/sepolicy/
$ adb push out/target/product/udoo/root/sepolicy /data/security/current/
sepolicy542 KB/s (86703 bytes in 0.155s)
$ adb shell setprop selinux.reload_policy 1
```

At this point, let's umount /ramdisk2 and remount it with the context= option:

```
root@udoo:/ # umount /ramdisk2/
root@udoo:/ # mount -t ramfs -osize=20m,context=u:object_r:ramdisk2:s0
ramfs /ramdisk2
```

Now, verify the contexts:

```
root@udoo:/ # ls -laZ | grep ramdisk
drwxr-xr-x root root u:object_r:ramdisk:s0 ramdisk
drwxr-xr-x root root u:object_r:ramdisk2:s0 ramdisk2
```

We can override the genfscon context with the mount option, context=<context>. In fact, if we look at dmesg, we can see some great messages. When we mounted ramfs without the context option, we got:

```
<7>SELinux: initialized (dev ramfs, type ramfs), uses genfs_contexts
```

When we mounted it with the context=<context> option, we got:

```
<7>SELinux: initialized (dev ramfs, type ramfs), uses mountpoint labeling
```

We can see that SELinux gives us some helpful messages while trying to figure out from where it sources its labels.

Now, let's go onto labeling filesystems with the xattr support, such as ext4. We will start with the toolbox command, chcon. The chcon command allows you to set the context of a file system object explicitly, it does not consult file_contexts.

Let's take a look at /system/bin and in it, at the first 10 files:

```
$ adb shell ls -laZ /system/bin | head -n10
-rwxr-xr-x root shell u:object_r:system_file:s0 InputDispatcher_test
-rwxr-xr-x root shell u:object_r:system_file:s0 InputReader_test
-rwxr-xr-x root shell u:object_r:system_file:s0 abcc
-rwxr-xr-x root shell u:object_r:system_file:s0 adb
-rwxr-xr-x root shell u:object_r:system_file:s0 am
-rwxr-xr-x root shell u:object_r:zygote_exec:s0 app_process
-rwxr-xr-x root shell u:object_r:system_file:s0 applypatch
-rwxr-xr-x root shell u:object_r:system_file:s0 applypatch_static
drwxr-xr-x root shell u:object_r:system_file:s0 asan
-rwxr-xr-x root shell u:object_r:system_file:s0 asanwrappe
```

We can see that many of them have the `system_file` label, which is the default label for that filesystem; let's change the `am` type to `am_exec`. Again, we need to create a new type by adding the following to `sepolicy` file, `file.te`:

```
type am_exec, file_type;
```

Now, rebuild the policy file, push it to the UDOO, and trigger a reload. After that, let's start remounting the system, since it is read only:

```
root@udoo:/ # mount -orw,remount /system
```

Now perform `chcon`:

```
root@udoo:/ # chcon u:object_r:am_exec:s0 /system/bin/am
```

Verify the result:

```
root@udoo:/ # la -laZ /system/bin/am
-rwxr-xr-x root shell u:object_r:am_exec:s0 am
```

Additionally, the `restorecon` command will use `file_contexts`, and restore that file to what is set in the `file_contexts` file, which should be `system_file`:

```
root@udoo:/ # restorecon /system/bin/am
root@udoo:/ # la -laZ /system/bin/am
-rwxr-xr-x root shell u:object_r:system_file:s0 am
```

As you can see, `restorecon` was able to consult `file_contexts` and restore the specified context on that object.

The Android system's filesystem gets constructed during the build time, and consequently, all its file objects are labeled during that process. We can also change this at build time by changing `file_contexts`. With this changed, the system partition rebuilt, and after reflashing the system, we should see the `am` file with the `am_exec` type. We can test this by amending the `sepolicy` file, `file_contexts` by adding this line at the end of the `system/bin` section:

```
/system/bin/am u:object_r:am_exec:s0
```

Rebuild the whole system with:

```
$ make -j8 2>&1 | tee logz
```

Now flash and reboot, and let's take a look at the `/system/bin/am` context as follows:

```
root@udoo:/ # ls -laZ /system/bin/am
-rwxr-xr-x root shell u:object_r:am_exec:s0 am
```

This shows that the system partition respects the file contexts for build-time labeling, and how we can control these labels.

Fixing up /data

Additionally in the audit logs, we have seen a bunch of unlabeled files, for instance, the following denial:

```
type=1400 msg=audit(86559.780:344): avc: denied { append } for
pid=2668 comm="UsbDebuggingHan" name="adb_keys" dev=mmcblk0p4 ino=42
scontext=u:r:system_server:s0 tcontext=u:object_r:unlabeled:s0
tclass=file
```

We can see that the device is mmcblk0p4, which mount commands and will tell us what filesystem this is mounted to, in its output:

root@udoo:/ # mount | grep mmcblk0p4

/dev/block/mmcblk0p4 /data ext4 rw,seclabel,nosuid,nodev,noatime,nodirati me,errors=panic,user_x0

So why does the /data filesystem have so many unlabeled files? The reason is that SELinux is meant to be turned on from an empty device, that is, from first boot. Android builds the data directory structures on demand. Thus, all the labels for the /data are handled by the file_contexts file since it is ext4. Also, it is handled by the systems that create the /data files and directories. These systems have been modified to label the data partition based on the file_contexts specifications. So this presents two options: wipe /data and reboot, or restorecon -R /data.

Option one is a bit harsh, but if you eject the SD card and remove all the files on the data partition, partition 4, Android will rebuild and you won't see any more unlabeled issues. However, this is not recommended for deployed devices when you upgrade; you will destroy all of the users' data.

Option two is more palatable in deployed scenarios, but has its limitations. Notably, executing restorecon -R /data will take a long time and must be done early in boot, right after the mount. However, this is really the only option at this point. Google, however, has done a lot of work in this area, and created a system that intelligently relabels /data on policy updates. For our use, we will choose a variant of option two, especially after considering how sparsely populated the /data filesystem is; we really haven't installed or generated a lot of user data yet. With that stated, execute:

root@udoo:/ # restorecon -R /data

root@udoo:/ # reboot

We don't have to execute `restorecon` early in boot since our system is in permissive mode, and we're not in a deployed scenario. Now, let's pull the `audit.log` file and compare it to the already pulled `audit.log`:

```
$ adb pull /data/misc/audit/audit.log audit_data_relabel.log
170 KB/s (14645 bytes in 0.084s)
```

Let's use `grep` to count the number of occurrences in each file:

```
$ grep -c unlabeled audit.log
185
$ grep -c unlabeled audit_data_relabel.log
0
```

Great, we fixed up all of our unlabeled issues on `/data`!

A side note on security

Note that even though we are running all these commands and changing all these things, this is not a security vulnerability within SELinux. Being able to change type labels, mounting filesystems, and associating filesystems with a type, all require allow rules. If you look through the audit logs, you'll see a slew of denials; a sample is provided:

```
type=1400 msg=audit(90074.080:192): avc: denied { associate } for
pid=3211 comm="touch" name="foo" scontext=u:object_r:ramdisk_
newfile:s0 tcontext=u:object_r:ramdisk:s0 tclass=filesystem
type=1400 msg=audit(90069.120:187): avc: denied { mount } for pid=3205
comm="mount" name="/" dev=ramfs ino=1992 scontext=u:r:init_shell:s0
tcontext=u:object_r:ramdisk:s0 tclass=filesystem
```

If we were in an enforcing mode, we wouldn't have been able to perform any of the experiments shown here.

Summary

In this chapter, we saw how to get files into contexts by relabeling them. We used a variety of techniques to accomplish this task, from toolbox commands such as `chcon` and `restorecon`, to mount options and dynamic transitions. With these tools, we can ensure that all filesystem objects are labeled correctly. This way, we end up with the right target contexts so that the policies we author are effective. In the next chapter, we will focus on the processes, making sure that they are in the right domain or context.

Adding Services to Domains

9

In the previous chapter, we covered the process of getting file objects in the proper domain. In most cases, the file object is the target. However, in this chapter, we will:

- Emphasize labeling processes — notably Android services that are run and managed by init
- Manage the services ancillary associated objects created by init

Init – the king of daemons

The init process is vital in a Linux system, and Android is not special in this case. However, Android has its own implementation of init. Init is the first process on the system, and thus has a **Process ID (PID)** of 1. All other processes are the result of a direct fork() from init, thus all processes eventually are parented under init, either directly or indirectly. Init is responsible for cleaning up and maintaining these processes. For instance, any child process whose parent dies is reparented under init by the kernel. In this way, init can call wait() (man 2 wait for more details) to clean up after the process when it exits.

 A process which has terminated but has not had wait() called is a **zombie** process. The kernel must keep the process data structures around until this call. Failing to do so will consume memory indefinitely.

Since init is the root of all processes, it also provides a mechanism to declare and execute commands through its own scripting language. Files using this language to control init are referred to as init scripts, and we have already modified some of them. In the source tree, we used the `init.rc` file, which you can reach by navigating to `device/fsl/imx6/etc/init.rc`, but on the device, it is packaged with the ramdisk at `/init.rc`, and is made available to init, which is also packaged in the ramdisk at `/init`.

To add a service to the init script, you can modify the `init.rc` file and add a declaration, as follows:

```
service <name> <path> [ <argument>... ]
```

Here, `name` is the service name, `path` is the path to the executable, and `argument` are space delimited argument strings to be delivered to the executable in its `argv` array.

For example, here is the service declaration for `rild`, the **Radio Interface Layer Daemon (RILD)**:

```
Service ril-daemon /system/bin/rild
```

It is often the case that additional service options can and need to be added. The init script `service` statement supports a rich assortment of options. For the complete list, refer to the informational file located at `system/core/init/readme.txt`. Additionally, we covered the SE for Android-specific changes in *Chapter 3, Android Is Weird*.

Continuing to dissect `rild`, we see that the rest of the declaration in the UDOO `init.rc` is as follows:

```
Service ril-daemon /system/bin/rild
    class main
    socket rild stream 660 root radio
    socket rild-debug stream 660 radio system
    socket rild-ppp stream 660 radio system
    user root
    group radio cache inet misc audio sdcard_rw log
```

The interesting thing to note here is that it creates quite a few sockets. The `socket` keyword in `init.rc` is described by the `readme.txt` file:

From the source tree file `system/core/init/readme.txt`:

socket <name> <type> <perm> [<user> [<group> [<context>]]]

Create a Unix domain socket named `/dev/socket/<name>` and pass its `fd` to the launched process. The type must be `dgram`, `stream`, or `seqpacket`. The `user` and `group` IDs default to 0. The SELinux security context for the socket is `context`. It defaults to the service security context, as specified by `seclabel`, or is computed based on the service executable file's security context.

Let's take a look at this directory and see what we've found.

```
root@udoo:/dev/socket # ls -laZ | grep adb
srw-rw---- system system u:object_r:adbd_socket:s0 adbd
```

This raises the question, "How did it get into that domain?" Using our knowledge from the previous chapter, we know that `/dev` is a `tmpfs`, so we know that it did not enter this domain through `xattrs`. It must be either a code modification or a type transition. Let's check whether it's a type transition. If it is, we would expect to see a statement in the expanded `policy.conf`. SELinux policy is based on the `m4` macro language. During builds, it is expanded into `policy.conf`, and then compiled. *Chapter 12, Mastering the Tool Chain*, has more details on this.

We can discover this by using sesearch to find type transitions for `adbd_socket`:

```
$ sesearch -T -t adbd_socket $OUT/sepolicy
```

As you can see from the empty output, there are zero such lines, so it's not the policy which is doing this but a code change.

In Linux, processes are created with `fork()` followed by `exec()`. Because of this, we are able to afford great keywords to search the init daemon. We suspect that the code to set up the socket is just after a call to `fork()` in the child processes and before a call to `exec()`:

```
$ grep -n fork system/core/init/init.c
235: pid = fork();
```

So, the fork we are searching for is on line 235 of init.c; let's open init.c in a text editor and take a look. We will find the following snippet to examine:

```
. . .
NOTICE("starting '%s'\n", svc->name);

  pid = fork();

  if (pid == 0) {
    struct socketinfo *si;
    struct svcenvinfo *ei;
    char tmp[32];
    int fd, sz;

    umask(077);
    if (properties_inited()) {
      get_property_workspace(&fd, &sz);
      sprintf(tmp, "%d,%d", dup(fd), sz);
      add_environment("ANDROID_PROPERTY_WORKSPACE", tmp);
    }

    for (ei = svc->envvars; ei; ei = ei->next)
      add_environment(ei->name, ei->value);

    for (si = svc->sockets; si; si = si->next) {
      int socket_type = (
        !strcmp(si->type, "stream") ? SOCK_STREAM :
          (!strcmp(si->type, "dgram") ? SOCK_DGRAM : SOCK_SEQPACKET));
      int s = create_socket(si->name, socket_type,
            si->perm, si->uid, si->gid, si->socketcon ?: scon);
      if (s >= 0) {
        publish_socket(si->name, s);
      }
  . . .
```

According to man 2 fork, the return code of fork() in the child process is 0. The child process executes within this if statement and the parent skips it. The function create_socket() also seems interesting. It appears to take the name of the service, the type of socket, permissions flags, uid, gid, and socketcon. What is socketcon? Let's check whether we can trace back to where it is set.

If we look before `fork()`, we can see that the parent process gets its `scon` based on two factors:

```
...
    if (svc->seclabel) {
      scon = strdup(svc->seclabel);
      if (!scon) {
        ERROR("Out of memory while starting '%s'\n", svc->name);
        return;
      }
    } else {
...
```

The first path through the `if` statement occurs when `svc->seclabel` is not null. This `svc` structure is populated with the options that can be associated with a service. As a refresher from *Chapter 3, Android Is Weird*, `seclabel` lets you explicitly set the context on a service, hardcoded to the value in init.rc. The `else` clause is a bit more involved and interesting.

In the `else` clause, we get the context of the current process by calling `getcon()`. This function, since we're running in init, should return `u:r:init:s0` and store it in `mycon`. The next function, `getfilecon()` is passed the path of the executable, and checks the context of the file itself. The third function is the workhorse here: `security_compute_create()`. This takes the `mycon`, `fcon`, and `target` class and computes the security context, `scon`. Given these inputs, it tries to determine, based on policy type transitions, what the resulting domain for the child should be. If no transitions are defined, `scon` will be the same as `mycon`.

A conditional expression within the `create_socket()` function additionally determines the socket context passed. The variable `si` is a structure that contains all the options to the socket statement in the init `service` section. As specified by the `readme.txt` file, `si->socketcon` is the socket context argument. In other words, the socket context can come from one of three places (in descending priority):

- The `socketcon` option on the socket option in the `service` declaration
- The `seclabel` option on the `service` keyword
- Dynamically computed from source and target contexts

The socket context is passed to `create_socket()`. Now, let's look at `create_socket()`. This function is defined at `system/core/init/util.c:87`. The snippets of code around `socket()` seem interesting:

```
    . . .
      if (socketcon)
        setsockcreatecon(socketcon);

      fd = socket(PF_UNIX, type, 0);
      if (fd < 0) {
        ERROR("Failed to open socket '%s': %s\n", name, strerror(errno));
        return -1;
      }

      if (socketcon)
        setsockcreatecon(NULL);
    . . .
```

The `setsockcreatecon()` function sets the process' socket creation context. This means that the socket created by the `socket()` call will have the context set via `setsockcreatecon()`. After it's created, the process resets it to the original by using `setsockcreatecon(NULL)`.

The next bit of interesting code is around `bind()`:

```
    . . .
      filecon = NULL;
      if (sehandle) {
        ret = selabel_lookup(sehandle, &filecon, addr.sun_path, S_IFSOCK);
        if (ret == 0)
          setfscreatecon(filecon);
      }

      ret = bind(fd, (struct sockaddr *) &addr, sizeof (addr));
      if (ret) {
        ERROR("Failed to bind socket '%s': %s\n", name, strerror(errno));
        goto out_unlink;
      }

      setfscreatecon(NULL);
      freecon(filecon);
    . . .
```

Here, we have set the file creation context. The functions are analogous to `setsock_creation()`, but work for filesystem objects. However, the `selabel_lookup()` function looks in `file_contexts` for the context of the file. The part you might be missing is that the call to `bind()`, for path-based sockets, creates a file at the path specified in `sockaddr_un struct`. So, the socket object and the filesystem node entry are distinctly separate things and can have different contexts. Typically, the socket belongs to the process' context, and the filesystem node is given some other context.

Dynamic domain transitions

We saw init computing of the contexts for the init sockets, but we never encountered it while setting the domains for child processes. In this section, we will dive into the two techniques to do so: explicit setting with an init script and sepolicy dynamic domain transitions.

The first way to the domains for child processes is with the `seclabel` statement in the init script service declaration. Within the child processes execution after `fork()`, we find this statement:

```
if (svc->seclabel) {
if (is_selinux_enabled() > 0 && setexeccon(svc->seclabel) < 0) {
ERROR("cannot setexeccon('%s'): %s\n", svc->seclabel,
strerror(errno));
_exit(127);
}
}
```

To clarify, the `svc` variable is the structure that contains the service options and arguments, so `svc->seclabel` is `seclabel`. If it's set, it calls `setexeccon()`, which sets the process' execution context for anything it executes via `exec()`. Further down, we see that the `exec()` function calls are made. The `exec()` syscall never returns on success; it only returns on failure.

The other way to set the domains for child processes, which is the preferred way, is by using sepolicy. It's preferred because the policy has no dependencies on anything else. By hardcoding a context into init, you're coupling a dependency between the init script and the sepolicy. For instance, if the sepolicy removes a type that was hardcoded in the init script, the init `setcon` will fail, but both systems will compile correctly. If you remove a type for a type transition and leave the transition statement, you can catch the error at compile time. Since we looked at the `rild` service statement, let's look at the `rild.te` policy file located in `sepolicy`. We should search for the `type_transition` keyword in this file using `grep`:

```
$ grep -c type_transition rild.te
0
```

No instances of `type_transition` are found, but this keyword must exist, similar to files. However, it can be hidden in an unexpanded macro. The SELinux policy files are in the m4 macro language, and they get expanded prior to being compiled. Let's look through `rild.te` and check whether we can find some macros. They are distinguished and look like functions with parameters. The first macro we come across is the `init_daemon_domain(rild)` macro. Now, we need to find this macro's definition in `sepolicy`. The m4 language uses the `define` keyword to declare macros, so we can search for that:

```
$ grep -n init_daemon_domain * | grep define
te_macros:99:define(`init_daemon_domain', `
```

Our macro is declared in `te_macros`, which coincidentally holds all the macros related to **type enforcement** (TE). Let's take a look at what this macro does in more detail. First, its definition is:

```
...
#####################################
# init_daemon_domain(domain)
# Set up a transition from init to the daemon domain
# upon executing its binary.
define(`init_daemon_domain', `
domain_auto_trans(init, $1_exec, $1)
tmpfs_domain($1)
')
...
```

The commented lines in the preceding code (lines starting with # in m4), state that it sets up a transition from init to the daemon domain. This sounds like something we want. However, both the encompassing statements are macros, and we need to recursively expand them. We will start with `domain_auto_trans()`:

```
...
#####################################
# domain_auto_trans(olddomain, type, newdomain)
# Automatically transition from olddomain to newdomain
# upon executing a file labeled with type.
#
define(`domain_auto_trans', `
# Allow the necessary permissions.
domain_trans($1,$2,$3)
# Make the transition occur by default.
type_transition $1 $2:process $3;
')
...
```

The comment here indicates that we are headed in the proper direction; however, we need to keep expanding macros in our search. According to the comment, the `domain_trans()` macro allows just the transition to occur. Remember that almost everything in SELinux needs explicit permission from the policy in order to happen, including type transitions. The last statement in the macro is the one we were searching for:

```
type_transition $1 $2:process $3;
```

If you expand this statement out, you'll get:

```
type_transition init rild_exec:process rild;
```

What this statement conveys is that if you make an `exec()` syscall on a file with the type `rild_exec`, and the executing domain is init, then make the child process' domain `rild`.

Explicit contexts via seclabel

The other option for setting contexts is very straightforward. It's hardcoding them with the init script in the `service` declaration. In the `service` declaration, as we saw in *Chapter 3, Android Is Weird*, there were modifications to the init language. One of the additions is `seclabel`. This option just lets init explicitly change the context of the service to the argument given to `seclabel`. Here is an example of `adbd`:

```
Service adbd /sbin/adbd
   class core
   socket adbd stream 660 system system
   disabled
   seclabel u:r:adbd:s0
```

So why use dynamic transitions on some and `seclabel` on others? The answer is dependent on where you're executing from. Things such as `adbd` execute early on from the ramdisk, and since the ramdisk really doesn't use per file labels, you can't set up transitions properly — the target has the same context.

Relabeling processes

Now that we are armed with dynamic process transitions, and the ability to set socket contexts from init scripts is needed. Let's attempt to relabel the services that are in improper contexts. We can tell if they're improper by checking them against the following rules:

- No other process but init should be in the init context
- No long running process should be in the init_shell domain
- Nothing but zygote should be in the zygote domain

 A more comprehensive test suite is part of CTS on AOSP. Refer to the Android CTS project for more details: (git clone) https://android.googlesource.com/platform/cts. Take note of the ./hostsidetests/security/src/android/cts/security/SELinuxHostTest.java and ./tests/tests/security/src/android/security/cts/SELinux.*.java tests.

Let's run some basic commands and evaluate the status of our UDOO over the adb connection:

```
$ adb shell ps -Z | grep init
u:r:init:s0 root 1 0 /init
u:r:init:s0 root 2267 1 /sbin/watchdogd
u:r:init_shell:s0 root 2278 1 /system/bin/sh
$ adb shell ps -Z | grep zygote
u:r:zygote:s0 root 2285 1 zygote
```

We have two processes in the improper domains. The first is watchdogd, and the second is a sh process. We need to find these and correct them.

We will start with the mystery sh program. As you can recall from the previous chapter, our UDOO serial console process had the context of init_shell, so this is a good suspect. Let's check PIDs and find out. From a UDOO serial console execute:

```
root@udoo:/ # echo $$
2278
```

We can compare this PID to the PID field in the adb shell ps output here (PID field is the third field, index 2), and as you can see, we have a match.

From there, we need to find the service declaration for this. We know that it is in
init.rc since it's running in init_shell, a type that can only be transitioned to
by init directly as per the SELinux policy. Also, init only starts processing things by
service declarations, so in order to be in init_shell, you must start by init via a
service declaration.

 Use sesearch to find out such things on the compiled sepolicy binary:
```
$ sesearch -T -s init -t shell_exec -c process $OUT/
root/sepolicy
```

If we search init.rc for the UDOO, which is in udoo/device/fsl/imx6/etc, we
can grep its contents for /system/bin/sh, the command in question. If we do that,
we will find:

```
$ grep -n "/system/bin/sh" init.rc
499:service console /system/bin/sh
702:service wifi_mac /system/bin/sh /system/etc/check_wifi_mac.sh
```

Let's look at 499 since we don't have anything to do with Wi-Fi:

```
service console /system/bin/sh
   class core
   console
   user root
   group root
```

If this is the service in question, we should be able to disable it, and verify that our
serial connection no longer works:

```
$ adb shell setprop ctl.stop console
```

My live serial connection died at:

```
root@udoo:/ # avc: denied { set } for property=ctl.console
scontext=u:r:shell:s0 tcontext=u:e
```

Now that we have verified what it is, we can start it back up:

```
$ adb shell setprop ctl.start console
```

With the system back in a working state, we now need to address the best way to correct the label on this service. We have two options:

- Using an explicit `seclabel` entry in `init.rc`
- Using a type transition

The option we will use here is the first. The reason is because init executes shell from time to time, and we don't want all of these in the console processes domain. We want least privilege to segregate the running processes. By using the explicit seclabel, we won't change any of the other shells that are executed along the way.

To do this, we need to modify the `init.rc` entry for console; add:

```
service console /system/bin/sh
  class core
  console
  user root
  group root
  seclabel u:r:shell:s0
```

The proper domain for this executable is `shell`, since it should have the same permission set as `adb shell`. After you make this change, recompile the bootimage, flash, and then reboot. We can see that it is now in a shell domain. To verify, execute the following from a UDOO serial connection:

```
root@udoo:/ # id -Z
uid=0(root) gid=0(root) context=u:r:shell:s0
```

Alternatively, execute the following command using `adb`:

```
$ adb shell ps -Z | grep "system/bin/sh"
u:r:shell:s0 root 2279 1 /system/bin/sh
```

The next one we need to take care of is `watchdogd`. The `watchdogd` process already has a domain and allows rules in `watchdog.te`; so we just need to add a `seclabel` statement and get it into this proper domain. Modify `init.rc`:

```
  # Set watchdog timer to 30 seconds and pet it every 10 seconds to get
  a 20 second margin
  service watchdogd /sbin/watchdogd 10 20
    class core
    seclabel u:r:watchdogd:s0
```

To verify using `adb`, execute the following command:

```
$ adb shell ps -Z | grep watchdog
u:r:watchdogd:s0 root 2267 1 /sbin/watchdogd
```

At this point, we have made actual policy corrections that the UDOO was in need of. However, we need to practice the use of dynamic domain transitions. A good teaching example would have subshells from a shell in their own domain. Let's start by defining a new domain and setting up the transition.

We will create a new `.te` file in `sepolicy` called `subshell.te`, and edit it so that its contents contain the following:

```
type subshell, domain, shelldomain, mlstrustedsubject;
# domain_auto_trans(olddomain, type, newdomain)
# Automatically transition from olddomain to newdomain
# upon executing a file labeled with type.
#
domain_auto_trans(shell, shell_exec, subshell)
```

Now, the `mmm` trick used earlier in the book can be used to compile just the policy Also, use `adb push` command to push the new policy to `/data/security/current/sepolicy` and execute `setprop` to reload the policy, just as we did in *Chapter 8, Applying Contexts to Files*.

To test this, we should be able to type `sh`, and verify the domain transition. We will start by getting our current context:

```
root@udoo:/ # id -Z
uid=0(root) gid=0(root) context=u:r:shell:s0
```

Then execute a shell by doing:

```
root@udoo:/ # sh
root@udoo:/ # id -Z
uid=0(root) gid=0(root) context=u:r:subshell:s0
```

We were able to use a dynamic type transition to get a new process in a domain. If you couple this with labeling files, as presented in *Chapter 8, Applying Contexts to Files,* you have a powerful tool to control process permissions.

Limitations on app labeling

A fundamental limitation of these dynamic process transitions is that they require an exec() system call to be made. Only then can SELinux compute the new domain, and trigger the context switch. The only other way to do this is by modifying the code, which essentially is what init is doing when you specify seclabel(). The init code sets the exec context for its process, causing the next exec to end up in the specified domain. In fact, we can see this in the init.c code:

```
if (svc->seclabel) {
if (is_selinux_enabled() > 0 && setexeccon(svc->seclabel) < 0) {
ERROR("cannot setexeccon('%s'): %s\n", svc->seclabel,
strerror(errno));
_exit(127);
}
}
```

Here, the child process gets its execute context set by a call to setexeccon() before the exec() system call hands over control to a new binary image. In Android, applications are not spawned this way, and no exec() syscall exists in the process creation path; so a new mechanism will be needed.

Summary

In this chapter, we learned how to label processes via type transitions as well as via the seclabel statements. We also investigated how init manages service sockets, and how to properly label them. We then corrected the process contexts for the serial console as well as the watchdog daemon.

Applications in Android never have an explicit call to exec() to start their program execution. Since there is no exec(), we have to label applications with a code change. In the next chapter, we will address how this happens, and how applications get labeled.

10
Placing Applications in Domains

In *Chapter 3*, *Android Is Weird*, we introduced the zygote and that all applications, APKs in Android speak, emanate from the zygote just like services emanate from the init process. As such, they need to be labeled, as we did in the previous chapter. Recall that labeling is the same as placing a process in a domain of that label. Applications need to be labeled as well.

 APK is the file extension and format for installable application packages on Android. It's analogous to the desktop package formats like RPM (Redhat based) or DEB (Debian based).

In this chapter, we will learn to:

- Properly label application private data directories and their runtime contexts
- Further examine zygote and methods to secure it
- Discover how a finished mac_permssions.xml file assigns seinfo value
- Create a new custom domain

The case to secure the zygote

Android applications with elevated permissions and capabilities are spawned from the zygote. An example of this is the system server, a large process comprised of native and non-native code hosting a variety of services. The system server houses the activity manager, package manager, GPS feeds and so on. The system server also runs with a highly sensitive UID of system (1000). Also, many OEMs package what are known as **system apps**, which are standalone applications running with the system UID.

The zygote also spawns applications that do not need elevated permissions. All third-party applications represent this. Third party applications run as their own UID, separate from sensitive UIDs, such as `system`. Additionally, applications get spawned into various UIDs such as `media`, `nfc`, and so on. OEMs tend to define additional UIDs.

It's important to note that to get into a special UID, like `system`, you must be signed with the proper key. Android has four major keys used to sign applications: `media`, `platform`, `shared`, and `testkey`. They are located in `build/target/product/security`, along with a `README`.

According to the `README`, the key usage is as follows:

- `testkey`: A generic key for packages that do not otherwise specify a key.
- `platform`: A test key for packages that are part of the core platform.
- `shared`: A test key for things that are shared in the home/contacts process.
- `media`: A test key for packages that are part of the media/download system.

In order to request `system` UID for your application, you must be signed with the `platform` key. Possession of the private key is required to execute in these more privileged environments.

As you can see, we have applications executing at a variety of permission levels, and trust levels. We cannot trust third party applications since they are created by unknown entities, and we can trust things signed with our private keys. However, before SELinux, application permissions were still bound by the same DAC permission limitations as those identified in *Chapter 1, Linux Access Controls*. Because of these properties, it makes the zygote a prime target for attack, as well as fortification with SELinux.

Fortifying the zygote

Now that we have identified a problem with zygote, the next step is understanding how to get applications into appropriate domains. We need either SELinux policy or code changes to place new processes into a domain. In *Chapter 9, Adding Services to Domains*, we covered dynamic domain transitions with init-based services and the end of the chapter mentions the importance of the `exec()` syscall in the "Limitations on App Labeling" section. This is the trigger on which dynamic domain transitions occur. If there is no `exec` in the path, we would have to rely on code changes. However, one also has to consider the signing key in this security model, and there is no way in pure SELinux policy language to express the key the process was signed with.

Rather than exploring the whole zygote, we can dissect the following patches that introduce application labeling into Android. Additionally, we can discover how the introduced design meets the requirements of respecting the signing key, working within the design of SELinux and the zygote.

Plumbing the zygote socket

In *Chapter 3*, *Android Is Weird*, we learned that the zygote listens for requests to spawn a new application from a socket. The first patch to examine is https://android-review.googlesource.com/#/c/31066/. This patch modifies three files in the base frameworks of Android. The first file is Process.java in the method startViaZygote(). This method is the main entry point for other methods with respect to building string arguments and passing them to the zygote with zygoteSendArgsAndGetResult(). The patch introduces a new argument called seinfo. Later on, we will see how this gets used. It appears that this patch is plumbing this new seinfo argument over the socket. Note that this code is called external to the zygote process.

The next file to look at in this patch is ZygoteConnection.java. This code executes from within the context. The patch starts off by declaring a string member variable peerContext in the ZygoteConnection class. In the constructor, this peerContext member is set to the value obtained from a call to SELinux.getPeerContext(mSocket.getFileDescriptor()).

Since the LocalSocket mSocket is a Unix domain socket under the hood, you can obtain the connected client's credentials. In this case, the call to getPeerContext() gets the client's security context, or in more formal terms, the process label. After the initialization, further down in method runOnce(), we see it being used in calls to applyUidSecurityPolicy and other apply*SecurityPolicy routines. The protected method runOnce() is called to read one start command from the socket and arguments. Eventually, after the apply*SecurityPolicy checks, it calls forkandSpecialize(). Each security policy check has been modified to use SELinux on top of the existing DAC security controls. If we review applyUidSecurityPolicy, we see they make the call:

```
boolean allowed = SELinux.checkSELinuxAccess(peerSecurityContext,
peerSecurityContext, "zygote", "specifyids");
```

This is an example of a userspace leveraging mandatory access controls in what is known as an object manager. Additionally, a security check has been added for the mysterious seinfo string in the applyseInfoSecurityPolicy() method. All the security checks here for SELinux specify the target class zygote. So if we look into sepolicy access_vectors, we see the added class zygote. This is a custom class for Android and defines all the vectors checked in the security checks.

The last file we'll consider from this patch is `ActivityManagerService.java`. The `ActivityManager` is responsible for starting applications and managing their lifecycles. It's a consumer of the `Process.start` API and needs to specify `seinfo`. This patch is simple, and for now, just sends `null`. Later, we will see the patch enabling its use.

The next patch, `https://android-review.googlesource.com/#/c/31063/`, executes within the context of the Android Dalvik VM and is coded in the VM zygote process space. The `forkAndSpecialize()` we saw in `ZygoteConnection` ends up in this native routine. It enters using `static pid_t forkAndSpecializeCommon(const u4* args, bool isSystemServer)`. This routine is responsible for creating the new process that becomes the application.

It begins with housekeeping code moving from Java to C and sets up the `niceName` and `seinfo` values as C-style strings. Eventually, the code calls `fork()` and the child process starts doing things, like executing `setgid` and `setuid`. The `uid` and `gid` values are specified to the zygote connection with the `Process.start` method. We also see a new call to `setSELinuxContext()`. As an aside, the order of these events is important here. If you set the SELinux context of the new process too early, the process would need additional capabilities in the new context to do things like `setuid` and `setgid`. However, those permissions are best left to the `zygote` domain, so the application domain we entered can be as minimal as possible.

Continuing, `setSELinuxContext` eventually calls `selinux_android_setcontext()`. Note that the `HAVE_SELINUX` conditional compilation macros were removed after this commit, but prior to the 4.3 release. Also note that `selinux_android_setcontext()` is defined in `libselinux`, so our journey will take us there. Here we see the mysterious `seinfo` is still being passed along.

The next patch to evaluate is `https://android-review.googlesource.com/#/c/39601/`. This patch actually passes a more meaningful `seinfo` value from the Java layer. Rather than being set to `null`, this patch introduces some parsing logic from an XML file, and passes this along to the `Process.start` method.

This patch modifies two major components: `PackageManager` and `installd`. `PackageManager` runs inside the `system_server`, and performs application installation. It maintains the state of all installed packages in the system. The second component, a service known as `installd`, is a very privileged root service that creates all the applications' private directories on disk. Rather than giving system server, and therefore `PackageManager`, the capability to create these directories, only `installd` has these permissions. Using this approach, even the system server cannot read data in your private data directories unless you make it world readable.

This patch is larger than the others, so we are only going to inspect the parts directly relevant to our discussion. We'll start by looking at `PackageManagerService.java`. This class is the package manager, proper for Android. In the constructor for `PackageManagerService()`, we see the addition of `mFoundPolicyFile = SELinuxMMAC.readInstallPolicy();`.

Based on the naming, we can conjecture that this method is looking for some type of policy configuration file, and if found, returns true, setting the `mFoundPolicyFile` member variable. We also see some calls to `createDataDirs` and `mInstaller.*` calls. These we can ignore, since those calls are headed to `installd`.

The next major portion adds the following:

```
if (mFoundPolicyFile) {
   SELinuxMMAC.assignSeinfoValue(pkg);
}
```

It's important to note that this code was added into the `scanPackageLI()` method. This method is called every time a package needs to be scanned for installation. So at a high level, if some policy file is found during service startup, then a `seinfo` value is assigned to the package.

The next file to look at is `ApplicationInfo.java`, a container class for maintaining meta information about a package. As we can see, the `seinfo` value is specified here for storage purposes. Additionally, there is some code for serializing and deserializing the class via the Android specific `Parcel` implementation.

At this point, we should have a closer look at the `SELinuxMMAC.java` code to confirm our understanding of what's going on. The class starts by declaring two locations for policy files.

```
// Locations of potential install policy files.
private static final File[] INSTALL_POLICY_FILE = {
   new File(Environment.getDataDirectory(), "system/mac_permissions.
xml"),
   new File(Environment.getRootDirectory(), "etc/security/mac_
permissions.xml"),
   null };
```

According to this, policy files can exist in two locations- /data/system/mac_ permissions.xml and /system/etc/security/mac_permissions.xml. Eventually, we see the call from PackageManagerService initialization to the method defined in the class readInstallPolicy(), which eventually reduces to a call of:

```
private static boolean readInstallPolicy(File[] policyFiles) {
  FileReader policyFile = null;
  int i = 0;
  while (policyFile == null && policyFiles != null && policyFiles[i]
!= null) {
     try {
       policyFile = new FileReader(policyFiles[i]);
       break;
     } catch (FileNotFoundException e) {
       Slog.d(TAG,"Couldn't find install policy " + policyFiles[i].
getPath());
     }
   i++;
   }
 ...
```

With policyFiles set to INSTALL_POLICY_FILE, this code uses the array to find a file at the specified locations. It is priority based, with the /data location taking precedence over /system. The rest of the code in this method looks like parsing logic and fills up two hash tables that were defined in the class declaration:

```
// Signature seinfo values read from policy.
private static final HashMap<Signature, String> sSigSeinfo =
new HashMap<Signature, String>();
// Package name seinfo values read from policy.
private static final HashMap<String, String> sPackageSeinfo =
new HashMap<String, String>();
```

The sSigSeinfo maps Signatures, or signing keys, to seinfo strings. The other map, sPackageSeinfo maps a package name to a string.

At this point, we can read some formatted XML from the mac_permissions.xml file and create internal mappings from signing key to seinfo and package name to seinfo.

The other call from PackageManagerService into this class came from void assignSeinfoValue(PackageParser.Package pkg).

Let's investigate what this method can do. It starts by checking if the application is system UID or a system installed app. In other words, it checks whether the application is a third-party application:

```
if (((pkg.applicationInfo.flags & ApplicationInfo.FLAG_SYSTEM) != 0)
||
((pkg.applicationInfo.flags & ApplicationInfo.FLAG_UPDATED_SYSTEM_APP)
!= 0)) {
```

This code has subsequently been dropped by Google, and was initially a requirement for merge. We can, however, continue our evaluation. The code loops over all the signatures in the package, and checks against the hash table. If it is signed with something in that map, it uses the associated `seinfo` value. The other case is that it matches by package name. In either case, the package's `ApplictionInfo` class `seinfo` value is updated to reflect this and be used elsewhere by `installd` and zygote application spawn:

```
// We just want one of the signatures to match.
for (Signature s : pkg.mSignatures) {
  if (s == null)
    continue;
  if (sSigSeinfo.containsKey(s)) {
    String seinfo = pkg.applicationInfo.seinfo = sSigSeinfo.get(s);
    if (DEBUG_POLICY_INSTALL)
      Slog.i(TAG, "package (" + pkg.packageName +
        ") labeled with seinfo=" + seinfo);
    return;
    }
}
  // Check for seinfo labeled by package.
  if (sPackageSeinfo.containsKey(pkg.packageName)) {
    String seinfo = pkg.applicationInfo.seinfo = sPackageSeinfo.
get(pkg.packageName);
    if (DEBUG_POLICY_INSTALL)
      Slog.i(TAG, "package (" + pkg.packageName +
        ") labeled with seinfo=" + seinfo);
    return;
    }
  }
}
```

As an aside, what is merged into mainline AOSP and what is maintained in the NSA Bitbucket repositories is a bit different. The NSA has additional controls in these policy files that can cause an application installation to abort. Google and the NSA are "forked" over this issue, so to speak. In the NSA versions of SELinuxMMAC.java, you can specify that applications matching a specific signature or package name are allowed to have certain sets of Android-level permissions. For instance, you can block all applications from being installed that request CAMERA permissions or block applications signed with certain keys. This also highlights how important it can be to find patches within large code bases and quickly come up to speed on how projects evolve, which can often seem daunting.

The last file in this patch for us to consider is ActivityManagerService.java. This patch replaces the null with app.info.seinfo. After all that work and all that plumbing, we finally have the mystical seinfo value fully parsed, associated per application package, and sent along to the zygote for use in selinux_android_setcontext().

Now it would benefit us to sit back and think about some of the properties we wanted to achieve in labeling applications. One of them is to somehow couple a security context with the application signing key, and this is precisely the main benefit of seinfo. This is a highly sensitive and trusted string associated value of a signing key. The actual contents of the string are arbitrary and dictated in mac_permissions.xml, which is the next stop on our adventure.

The mac_permissions.xml file

The mac_permissions.xml file has a very confusing name. Expanded, the name is MAC permissions. However, its major mainline functionality is to map a signing key to a seinfo string. Secondarily, it can also be used to configure a non-mainstream install-time permission-checking feature, known as install time MMAC. MMAC controls are part of the NSA's work to implement mandatory access controls in the middleware layer. MMAC stands for "Middleware Mandatory Access Controls". Google has not merged any of the MMAC features. However, since we used the NSA Bitbucket repositories, our code base contains these features.

The mac_permissions.xml is an XML file, and should adhere to the following rules, where italicized portions are only supported on NSA branches:

- A signature is a hex encoded X.509 certificate and is required for each signer tag.
- A <signer signature="" > element may have multiple child elements:
    - ° allow-permission: It produces a set of maximal allowed permissions (whitelist)
    - ° deny-permission: It produces a blacklist of permissions to deny
    - ° allow-all: It is a wildcard tag that will allow every permission requested
    - ° package: It is a complex tag which defines allow, deny, and wildcard sub-elements for a specific package name protected by the signature
- Zero or more global <package name=""> tags are allowed. These tags allow a policy to be set outside any signature for specific package names.
- A <default> tag is allowed that can contain install policy for all apps not signed with a previously listed cert and not having a per package global policy.
- Unknown tags at any level are skipped.
- Zero or more signer tags are allowed.
- Zero or more package tags are allowed per signer tag.
- A <package name=""> tag may not contain another <package name=""> tag. If found, it's skipped.
- When multiple sub-elements appear for a tag, the following logic is used to ultimately determine the type of enforcement:
    - ° A blacklist is used if at least one deny-permission tag is found.
    - ° A whitelist is used, if not a blacklist, and at least one allow-permission tag is found.
    - ° A wildcard (accept all permissions) policy is used if not a blacklist and not a whitelist, and at least one allow-all tag is present.
    - ° If a <package name=""> sub-element is found, then that sub-element's policy is used according to the earlier logic and overrides any signature global policy type.
    - ° In order for a policy stanza to be enforced, at least one of the preceding situations must apply. Meaning, empty signer, default or package tags will not be accepted.

- Each `signer/default/package` (global or attached to a signer) tag is allowed to contain one `<seinfo value=""/>` tag. This tag represents additional info that each app can use in setting an SELinux security context on the eventual process.

- Strict enforcing of any XML stanza is not enforced in most cases. This mainly applies to duplicate tags, which are allowed. In the event that a tag already exists, the original tag is replaced.

- There are also no checks on the validity of permission names. Although valid Android permissions are expected, nothing prevents unknowns.

- Following are the enforcement decisions:

  - All signatures used to sign an app are checked for policy according to signer tags. However, only one of the signature policies has to pass.

  - In the event that none of the signature policies pass, or none even match, then a global package policy is sought. If found, this policy mediates the install.

  - The default tag is consulted last, if needed.

  - A local package policy always overrides any parent policy.

  - If none of the cases apply, then the app is denied.

The following examples ignore the Install MMAC support and focus on the mainline usage of `seinfo` mapping. The following is an example of stanza mapping all things signed with the platform key to `seinfo` value platform:

```
<!-- Platform dev key in AOSP -->
<signer signature="@PLATFORM" >
  <seinfo value="platform" />
</signer>
```

Here is an example mapping all things signed with the release key to the release domain with the exception of the browser. The browser gets assigned a `seinfo` value of `browser`, as follows:

```
<!-- release dev key in AOSP -->
<signer signature="@RELEASE" >
  <seinfo value="release" />
  <package name="com.android.browser" >
  <seinfo value="browser" />
  </package>
</signer>
...
```

Anything with an unknown key, gets mapped to the default tag:

```
...
<!-- All other keys -->
<default>
  <seinfo value="default" />
</default>
```

The signing tags are of interest, the @PLATFORM and @RELEASE are special processing strings used during build. Another mapping file maps these to actual key values. The file that is processed and placed onto the device has all key references replaced with hex encoded public keys rather than these placeholders. It also has all whitespace and comments stripped to reduce size. Let's take a look by pulling the built file from the device and formatting it.

```
$ adb pull /system/etc/security/mac_permissions.xml
$ xmllint --format mac_permissions.xml
```

Now, scroll to the top of the formatted output; you should see the following:

```
<?xml version="1.0" encoding="iso-8859-1"?>
<!-- AUTOGENERATED FILE DO NOT MODIFY -->
<policy>
  <signer signature="308204ae30820396a003020102020900d2cba57296ebebe23
00d06092a864886f70d0101050500308196310b30090603550406130255533113 3...
dec513c8443956b7b0182bcf1f1d">
    <allow-all/>
    <seinfo value="platform"/>
  </signer>
```

Notice that `signature=@PLATFORM` is now a hex string. This hex string is a valid X509 certificate.

keys.conf

The actual magic doing the mapping from `signature=@PLATFORM` in `mac_permissions.xml` is `keys.conf`. This configuration file allows you to map a pem encoded x509 to an arbitrary string. The convention is to start them with @, but this is not enforced. The format of the file is based on the Python config parser and contains sections. The section names are the tags in the `mac_permissions.xml` file you wish to replace with key values. The platform example is:

```
[@PLATFORM]
ALL : $DEFAULT_SYSTEM_DEV_CERTIFICATE/platform.x509.pem
```

In Android, when you build, you can have three levels of builds: `engineering`, `userdebug`, or `user`. In the `keys.conf` file, you can associate a key to be used for all levels with the section attribute `ALL`, or you can assign different keys per level. This is helpful when building release or user builds with very special release keys. We see an example of this in the `@RELEASE` section:

```
[@RELEASE]
ENG        : $DEFAULT_SYSTEM_DEV_CERTIFICATE/testkey.x509.pem
USER       : $DEFAULT_SYSTEM_DEV_CERTIFICATE/testkey.x509.pem
USERDEBUG  : $DEFAULT_SYSTEM_DEV_CERTIFICATE/testkey.x509.pem
```

The file also allows the use of environment variables through the traditional $ special character. The default location for the pem files is `build/target/product/security`. However, you should *never* use these keys for a user release build. These keys are the AOSP test keys and are public! By doing so, anyone can use the system key to sign their app and gain system privilege. The `keys.conf` file is only used during the build and is not located on the system.

seapp_contexts

So far, we have looked at how a finished `mac_permssions.xml` file assigns the `seinfo` value. Now we should address how the labeling is actually configured and utilizes this value. The labeling of applications is managed in another configuration file, `seapp_contexts`. Like `mac_permissions.xml`, it is loaded to the device. However, the default location is `/seapp_contexts`. The format of `seapp_contexts` is the `key=value` pair mappings per line, adhering to the following rules:

- Input selectors:
    - `isSystemServer` (boolean)
    - `user` (string)
    - `seinfo` (string)
    - `name` (string)
    - `sebool` (string)

- Input selector rules:
    - `isSystemServer=true` can only be used once.
    - An unspecified `isSystemServer` defaults to false.
    - An unspecified string selector will match any value.
    - A user string selector that ends in `*` will perform a prefix match.

- ° `user=_app` will match any regular app UID.
- ° `user=_isolated` will match any isolated service UID.
- ° All specified input selectors in an entry must match (logical AND).
- ° Matching is case-insensitive.
- ° Precedence rules in order:
  - ° `isSystemServer=true` before `isSystemServer=false`
  - ° Specified `user=` string before unspecified `user=` string
  - ° Fixed the `user=` string before the `user=` prefix (ending in `*`)
  - ° Longer `user=` prefix before shorter `user=` prefix
  - ° Specified `seinfo=` string before unspecified `seinfo=` string.
  - ° Specified `name=` string before unspecified `name=` string.
  - ° Specified `sebool=` string before unspecified `sebool=` string.

- **Outputs:**
  - ° `domain` (string): It specifies the process domain for the application.
  - ° `type` (string): It specifies the disk label for the applications' private data directory.
  - ° `levelFrom` (string; one of `none`, `all`, `app`, or `user`): It gives the MLS specifier.
  - ° `level` (string): It shows the hardcoded MLS value.

- **Output rules:**
  - ° Only entries that specify `domain=` will be used for app process labeling.
  - ° Only entries that specify `type=` will be used for app directory labeling.
  - ° `levelFrom=user` is only supported for `_app` or `_isolated` UIDs.
  - ° `levelFrom=app` or `levelFrom=all` is only supported for `_app` UIDs.
  - ° `level` may be used to specify a fixed level for any UID.

During application spawn, this file is used by the `selinux_android_setcontext()` and `selinux_android_setfilecon2()` functions to look up the proper application domain or filesystem context, respectively. The source for these can be found in `external/libselinux/src/android.c` and are recommended reads. For example, this entry places all applications with UID `bluetooth` in the `bluetooth` domain with a data directory label of `bluetooth_data_file`:

```
user=bluetooth domain=bluetooth type=bluetooth_data_file
```

This example places all third party or "default" applications into a process domain of `untrusted_app` and a data directory of `app_data_file`. It additionally uses MLS categories of `levelFrom=app` to help provide additional MLS-based separations.

```
user=_app domain=untrusted_app type=app_data_file levelFrom=app
```

Currently, this feature is experimental as this breaks some known application compatibility issues. At the time of this writing, this was a hot item of focus for both Google and NSA engineers. Since it is experimental, let's validate its functionality and then disable it.

We have not installed any third party applications yet, so we'll need to do so in order to experiment. FDroid is a useful place to find third party applications, so let's download something from there and install it. We can use the `0xbenchmark` application located at `https://f-droid.org/repository/browse/?fdid=org.zeroxlab.zeroxbenchmark` with an APK at `https://f-droid.org/repo/org.zeroxlab.zeroxbenchmark_9.apk`, as follows:

```
$ wget https://f-droid.org/repo/org.zeroxlab.zeroxbenchmark_9.apk
$ adb install org.zeroxlab.zeroxbenchmark_9.apk
567 KB/s (1193455 bytes in 2.052s)
pkg: /data/local/tmp/org.zeroxlab.zeroxbenchmark_9.apk
Success
```

> Check `logcat` for the install time `seinfo` value:
> ```
> $ adb logcat | grep SELinux
> I/SELinuxMMAC( 2557): package (org.zeroxlab.
> zeroxbenchmark) installed with seinfo=default
> ```

From your UDOO, launch the `0xbenchmark` APK. We should see it running with its label in `ps`:

```
$ adb shell ps -Z | grep untrusted
u:r:untrusted_app:s0:c40,c256 u0_a40 17890 2285 org.zeroxlab.
zeroxbenchmark
```

Notice the level portion of the context string `s0:c40,c256`. These categories were created with the `level=app` setting from `seapp_contexts`.

To disable it, we could simply remove the key-value pair for level from the entry in `seapp_contexts`, or we could leverage the `sebool` conditional assignment. Let's use the Boolean approach. Modify the sepolicy `seapp_contexts` file so the existing `untrusted_app` entry is modified, and a new one is added. Change `user=_app domain=untrusted_app type=app_data_file` to `user=_app sebool=app_level domain=untrusted_app type=app_data_file levelFrom=app`.

Build that with `mmm external/sepolicy`, as follows:

```
Error:
out/host/linux-x86/bin/checkseapp -p out/target/product/udoo/obj/ETC/
sepolicy_intermediates/sepolicy -o out/target/product/udoo/obj/ETC/seapp_
contexts_intermediates/seapp_contexts out/target/product/udoo/obj/ETC/
seapp_contexts_intermediates/seapp_contexts.tmp
Error: Could not find selinux boolean "app_level" on line: 42 in file:
out/target/product/udoo/obj/ETC/seapp_contexts_intermediates/seapp_
contexts
Error: Could not validate
```

Well, there was a build error complaining about not finding the `selinux` Boolean on line 42 of `seapp_contexts`. Let's attempt to correct the issue by declaring the Boolean. In `app.te`, add: `bool app_level false;`. Now push the newly built `seapp_contexts` and sepolicy file to the device and trigger a dynamic reload:

```
$ adb push $OUT/root/sepolicy /data/security/current/
$ adb push $OUT/root/seapp_contexts /data/security/current/
$ adb shell setprop selinux.reload_policy 1
```

We can verify that the Boolean exists by:

```
$ adb shell getsebool -a | grep app_level
app_level --> off
```

Due to design limitations, we need to uninstall and reinstall the application:

```
$ adb uninstall org.zeroxlab.zeroxbenchmark
```

Re-install and check the context of the process *after* launching it:

```
$ adb shell ps -Z | grep untrusted
u:r:untrusted_app:s0:c40,c256 u0_a40 17890 2285 org.zeroxlab.
zeroxbenchmark
```

Great! It failed. After some debugging, we discovered the source of the issue is that the path /data/security is not world searchable, causing a DAC permissions failure.

 We found this by printing off the result and error codes in android.c where we saw the fopen on seapp_contexts_file[] array (files in priority order) while checking the result of fp = fopen(seapp_contexts_file[i++], "r") in selinux_ android_seapp_context_reload() and using selinux_log() to dump the data to logcat.

```
$ adb shell ls -la /data | grep security
drwx------ system system 1970-01-04 00:22 security
```

Remember the set selinux context occurs after the UID switch, so we need to make it searchable for others. We can fix the permissions on the UDOO init.rc script by changing device/fsl/imx6/etc/init.rc. Specifically, change the line mkdir / data/security 0700 system system to mkdir /data/security 0711 system system. Build and flash the bootimage, and try the context test again.

```
$ adb uninstall org.zeroxlab.zeroxbenchmark
$ adb install ~/org.zeroxlab.zeroxbenchmark_9.apk
<launch apk>
$ adb shell ps -Z | grep org.zeroxlab.zeroxbenchmark
u:r:untrusted_app:s0 u0_a40 3324 2285 org.zeroxlab.zeroxbenchmark
```

So far, we've demonstrated how to use the sebool option on seapp_contexts to disable the MLS categories. It's important to note that when changing categories or types on APKs, it is required to remove and install the APK, or you will orphan the process from its data directory because it won't have access permissions under most circumstances.

Next, let's take this APK, uninstall it, and assign it a unique domain by changing its seinfo string. Typically, you use this feature to take a set of applications signed with a common key and get them into a custom domain to do custom things. For example, if you're an OEM, you may need to allow custom permissions to third party applications that are not signed with an OEM controlled key. Start by uninstalling the APK:

```
$ adb uninstall org.zeroxlab.zeroxbenchmark
```

Create a new entry in `mac_permissions.xml` by adding:

```
<signer signature="@BENCHMARK" >
<allow-all />
<seinfo value="benchmark" />
</signer>
```

Now we need to get a pem file for `keys.conf`. So unpackage the APK and extract the public certificate:

```
$ mkdir tmp
$ cd tmp
$ unzip ~/org.zeroxlab.zeroxbenchmark_9.apk
$ cd META-INF/
$ $ openssl pkcs7 -inform DER -in *.RSA -out CERT.pem -outform
PEM  -print_certs
```

We'll have to strip any cruft from the generated `CERT.pem` file. If you open it up, you should see these lines at the top:

```
subject=/C=UK/ST=ORG/L=ORG/O=fdroid.org/OU=FDroid/CN=FDroid
issuer=/C=UK/ST=ORG/L=ORG/O=fdroid.org/OU=FDroid/CN=FDroid
-----BEGIN CERTIFICATE-----
MIIDPDCCAiSgAwIBAgIEUVJuojANBgkqhkiG9w0BAQUFADBgMQswCQYDVQQGEwJV
SzEMMAoGA1UECBMDT1JHMQwwCgYDVQQHEwNPUkcxEzARBgNVBAoTCmZkcm9pZC5v
...
```

They need to be removed, so remove *only* the subject and issuer lines. The file should start with `BEGIN CERTIFICATE` and end with `END CERTIFICATE` scissor lines.

Let's move this to a new folder in our workspace called `certs` and move the certificate into this folder with a better name:

```
$ mkdir UDOO_SOURCE_ROOT/certs
$ mv CERT.pem UDOO_SOURCE_ROOT/certs/benchmark.x509.pem
```

We can set up our `keys.conf` by adding:

```
[@BENCHMARK]
ALL : certs/benchmark.x509.pem
```

Don't forget to update `seapp_contexts` in order to use the new mapping:

```
user=_app seinfo=benchmark domain=benchmark_app type=benchmark_app_data_
file
```

Now declare the new types to be used. The domain type should be declared in a file called `benchmark_app.te` in `sepolicy`:

```
# Declare the new type
type benchmark_app, domain;
# This macro adds it to the untrusted app domain set and gives it some
allow rules
# for basic functionality as well as object access to the type in
argument 2.
untrustedapp_domain(benchmark_app, benchmark_app_data_file)
```

Also, add the `benchmark_app_data_file` in `file.te`:

```
type benchmark_app_data_file, file_type, data_file_type, app_public_data_
type;
```

 You may not always want *all* of these attributes, especially if you're doing something security critical. Make sure you look at each attribute and macro and see its usage. You don't want to open up an unintended hole by having an overly permissive domain.

Rebuild the policy, push the required pieces, and trigger a reload.

```
$ mmm external/sepolicy/
$ adb push $OUT/system/etc/security/mac_permissions.xml /data/security/
current/
$ adb push $OUT/root/sepolicy /data/security/current/
$ adb push $OUT/root/seapp_contexts /data/security/current/
$ adb shell setprop selinux.reload_policy 1
```

Start a shell and grep logcat to see the `seinfo` value the benchmark APK is installed as. Then install the APK:

```
$ adb install ~/org.zeroxlab.zeroxbenchmark_9.apk
$ adb logcat | grep -i SELinux
```

On the `logcat` output, you should see:

```
I/SELinuxMMAC( 2564): package (org.zeroxlab.zeroxbenchmark) installed
with seinfo=default
```

It should have been `seinfo=benchmark`! What could have happened?

The problem is in `frameworks/base/services/java/com/android/server/pm/SELinuxMMAC.java`. It looks in `/data/security/mac_permissions.xml`; so we can just push `mac_permissions.xml`. This is another bug in the dynamic policy reload and has to do with historical changes in this loading procedure. The culprit is within the `frameworks/base/services/java/com/android/server/pm/SELinuxMMAC.java` file:

```
private static final File[] INSTALL_POLICY_FILE = {
new File(Environment.getDataDirectory(), "security/mac_permissions.xml"),
new File(Environment.getRootDirectory(), "etc/security/mac_permissions.xml"),
null};
```

To get around this, remount `system` and push it to the default location.

```
$ adb remount
$ adb push $OUT/system/etc/security/mac_permissions.xml /system/etc/security/
```

This does *not* require a `setprop selinux.reload_policy 1`. Uninstall and reinstall the benchmark APK, and check the logs:

```
I/SELinuxMMAC( 2564): package (org.zeroxlab.zeroxbenchmark) installed with seinfo=default
```

OK. It still didn't work. When we examined the code, the `mac_permissions.xml` file was loaded during package manager service start. This file won't get reloaded without a reboot, so let's uninstall the benchmark APK, and reboot the UDOO. After it's been booted and `adb` is enabled, trigger a dynamic reload, install the APK, and check `logcat`. It should have:

```
I/SELinuxMMAC( 2559): package (org.zeroxlab.zeroxbenchmark) installed with seinfo=benchmark
```

Now let's verify the process domain by launching the APK, checking `ps`, and verifying its application private directory:

```
<launch apk>
$ adb shell ps -Z | grep org.zeroxlab.zeroxbenchmark
u:r:benchmark_app:s0 u0_a45 3493 2285 org.zeroxlab.zeroxbenchmark
$ adb shell ls -Z /data/data | grep org.zeroxlab.zeroxbenchmark
drwxr-x--x u0_a45 u0_a45 u:object_r:benchmark_app_data_file:s0 org.zeroxlab.zeroxbenchmark
```

This time, all the types check out. We successfully created a new custom domain.

Summary

In this chapter, we investigated how to properly label application private data directories as well as their runtime contexts via the configuration files and SELinux policy. We also looked into the subsystems and code to make all of this work as well as some basic things that may go wrong along the way. In the next chapter, we will expand on how the policy and configuration files get built by peering into the SE for Android build system.

11
Labeling Properties

In this chapter, we will cover how to label properties via the `property_contexts` file.

Properties are a unique Android feature we learned about in *Chapter 3, Android Is Weird*. We want to label these to restrict setting of our properties to only the domains that should set them, preventing a classic DAC root attack from inadvertently changing the value. In this chapter, we will learn to:

- Create new properties
- Label new and existing properties
- Interpret and deal with property denials
- Enumerate special Android properties and their behaviors

Labeling via property_contexts

All properties are labeled using the `property_contexts` file, and its syntax is similar to `file_contexts`. However, instead of working on file paths, it works on property names or property keys (properties in Android are a key-value store). The property keys themselves are typically delimited with periods (`.`). This is analogous to `file_contexts`, except the slash (`/`) becomes a period. Some sample properties and their entries in `property_contexts` would look like the following:

```
ctl.ril-daemon  u:object_r:ctl_rildaemon_prop:s0
ctl.    u:object_r:ctl_default_prop:s0
```

Notice how all `ctl.` properties are labeled with the `ctl_default_prop` type, but `ctl.ril-daemon` has a different type label of `ctl_rildaemon_prop`. These are representative of how you can start generically and move to more specific values/types as necessary.

Additionally, anything not explicitly labeled defaults to default_prop through a "match all" expression in property_contexts:

```
# default property context
* u:object_r:default_prop:s0
```

Permissions on properties

One can view the current properties on the system, and create new ones with the command line utilities getprop and setprop, as shown in the following code snippet:

root@udoo:/ # getprop

...

[sys.usb.state]: [mtp,adb]

[wifi.interface]: [wlan0]

[wlan.driver.status]: [unloaded]

Recall from *Chapter 3, Android Is Weird*, that properties are mapped into everyone's address space, thus anyone can read them. However, not everyone can set (write) them. The DAC permission model for properties is hardcoded into system/core/init/property_service.c:

```
/* White list of permissions for setting property services. */
struct {
  const char *prefix;
  unsigned int uid;
  unsigned int gid;
} property_perms[] = {
  { "net.rmnet0.", AID_RADIO, 0 },
  { "net.gprs.", AID_RADIO, 0 },
  { "net.ppp", AID_RADIO, 0 },
  ...
  { "persist.service.bdroid.", AID_BLUETOOTH, 0 },
  { "selinux." , AID_SYSTEM, 0 },
  { "persist.audio.device", AID_SYSTEM, 0 },
  { NULL, 0, 0 }
```

You must have the UID or GID in the property_perms array to set any property that the prefix matches with. For instance, in order to set the selinux. properties, you must be UID AID_SYSTEM (uid 1000) or root. Yes, root can always set a property, and this is a key benefit to applying SELinux to Android properties. Unfortunately, there is no way to getprop -Z to list the properties and their labels, like with ls -Z and files.

Relabeling existing properties

In order to become more comfortable with labeling properties, let's relabel the `wifi.interface` property. First, let's verify its context by causing a denial and viewing the denial log, as shown in the following code:

```
root@udoo:/ # setprop wifi.interface wlan0
avc: denied { set } for property=wifi.interface scontext=u:r:shell:s0
tcontext=u:object_r:default_prop:s0 tclass=property_service
```

An interesting action occurred when we executed the `setprop` command over the UDOO serial console. The AVC denial record was printed out. This is because the serial console includes anything printed from the kernel using `printk()`. What happens here is the `init` process, which controls `setprops` as detailed in *Chapter 3, Android Is Weird,* writes a message to the kernel log. This log message shows up when we execute our `setprop` command. If you run this through `adb shell`, you'll see the message on the serial console, but not in the `adb` console. To do this, however, you must reboot your system because SELinux only prints denial records once while in permissive mode.

The command using `adb shell` is as follows:

```
$ adb shell setprop wifi.interface wlan0
```

The command using the serial console is as follows:

```
root@udoo:/ # avc: denied {set} for property=wifi.interface
scontext=u:r:shell:s0 tcontext=u:object_r:default_prop
usb 2-1.3: device descriptor read/64, error -110
```

From the denial output, we can see that the property type label is `default_prop`. Let's change this to `wifi_prop`.

We start by editing `property.te` in the `sepolicy` directory to declare the new type to label these properties by appending the following line:

```
type wifi_prop, property_type;
```

With the type declared, the next step is to apply the label by modifying `property_contexts` by adding the following:

```
# wifi properties
wifi. u:object_r:wifi_prop:s0
```

Build the policy, as follows:

```
$ mmm external/sepolicy
```

Push the new `property_contexts` file:

```
$ adb push out/target/product/udoo/root/property_contexts /data/security/
current
51 KB/s (2261 bytes in 0.042s)
```

Trigger a dynamic reload:

```
$ adb shell setprop selinux.reload_policy 1
# setprop wifi.interface wlan0
avc: denied { set } for property=wifi.interface scontext=u:r:shell:s0
tcontext=u:object_r:default_prop:s0 tclass=property_service
```

Ok, that didn't work! The `property_contexts` file must be in `/data/security`, not `/data/security/current`.

To discover this, search the `libselinux/src/android.c` file. There is no mention of `property_contexts` in this file; thus, it must be mentioned elsewhere. This leads us to search `system/core`, which contains the property service for uses of that file. The matches are on code in `init.c` to load the file from priority locations.

```
$ grep -rn property_contexts *
init/init.c:745: { SELABEL_OPT_PATH, "/data/security/property_contexts"
},
init/init.c:746: { SELABEL_OPT_PATH, "/property_contexts" },
init/init.c:760: ERROR("SELinux: Could not load property_contexts: %s\n",
```

Let's push the `property_contexts` file to the proper location and try again:

```
$ adb push out/target/product/udoo/root/property_contexts /data/security
51 KB/s (2261 bytes in 0.042s)
$ adb shell setprop selinux.reload_policy 1
root@udoo:/ # setprop wifi.interface wlan0
avc: received policyload notice (seqno=3)
init: sys_prop: permission denied uid:0 name:wifi.interface
```

Wow! It failed yet again. This exercise was meant to point out how tricky this can be if you forget to do something. No informative denial messages were displayed, only an indicator that it *was* denied. This is because the `sepolicy` file that contains the type declaration for `wifi_prop` was never pushed. This causes `check_mac_perms()` in `system/core/init/property_service.c` to fail in the `selinux_check_access()` function because it cannot find the type to compute the access check against, even though the look up in `property_contexts` succeeded. There are no verbose error logs from this.

We can correct this by ensuring that the `sepolicy` is pushed as well:

```
$ adb push out/target/product/udoo/root/sepolicy /data/security/current/
550 KB/s (87385 bytes in 0.154s)
$ adb shell setprop selinux.reload_policy 1
root@udoo:/ # setprop wifi.interface wlan0
avc: received policyload notice (seqno=4)
avc: denied { set } for property=wifi.interface scontext=u:r:shell:s0
tcontext=u:object_r:wifi_prop:s0 tclass=property_service
```

Now we see a denial message, as expected, but the label of the target (or property) is `u:object_r:wifi_prop:s0`.

Now with the target property labeled, you can allow access to it. Note that this is a contrived example, and in the real world, you probably would *not* want to allow access from shell to most properties. The policy should align with your security goals and the property of least privilege.

We can add an `allow` rule in `shell.te` in the following way:

```
# wifi prop
allow shelldomain wifi_prop:property_service set;
```

Compile the policy, push it to the phone, and trigger a dynamic reload:

```
$ mmm external/sepolicy/
$ adb push out/target/product/udoo/root/sepolicy /data/security/current/
547 KB/s (87397 bytes in 0.155s)
$ adb shell setprop selinux.reload_policy 1
```

Now attempt to set the `wifi.interface` property and notice the lack of denial.

```
root@udoo:/ # setprop wifi.interface wlan0
avc: received policyload notice (seqno=5)
```

Creating and labeling new properties

All properties are dynamically created in the system using `setprop` calls or function calls that do the equivalent from C (`bionic/libc/include/sys/system_properties.h`) and Java (`android.os.SystemProperties`). Note that the `System.getProperty()` and `System.setProperty()` Java calls work on application private property stores and are not tied into the global one.

For DAC controls, you need to modify `property_perms[]` as noted earlier to have permissions for non-root users to create or set the property. Note that root can always `set` and `create`, unless constrained by SELinux policy.

Suppose we want to create the `udoo.name` and `udoo.owner` properties; we only want the root user and shell domain to access them. We could create them like this:

```
root@udoo:/ # setprop udoo.name udoo
avc: denied { set } for property=udoo.name scontext=u:r:shell:s0
tcontext=u:object_r:default_prop:s0 tclass=property_service
root@udoo:/ # setprop udoo.owner William
```

Notice the denial shows these as being `default_prop` type. To correct this, we would relabel these, exactly as we did in the preceding section, *Relabeling existing properties*.

Special properties

In Android, there are some special properties that have different behaviors. We enumerate the property names and meanings in the proceeding sections.

Control properties

Properties that start with `ctl` are reserved as control properties for controlling services through `init`:

- `start`: Starts a service (`setprop ctl.start <servicename>`)
- `stop`: Stops a service (`setprop ctl.stop <servicename>`)
- `restart`: Restarts a service (`setprop ctl.restart <servicename>`)

Persistent properties

Any property starting with the prefix `persist` persists across reboots and is restored. The data is saved to `/data/property` in files of the same name as the property.

```
root@udoo:/ # ls /data/property/
persist.gps.oacmode
persist.service.bdroid.bdaddr
persist.sys.profiler_ms
persist.sys.usb.config
```

SELinux properties

The `selinux.reload_policy` property is special. As we have seen, its use is for triggering a dynamic reload event.

Summary

In this chapter, we have examined how to create and label new and existing properties and some of the oddities that occur when doing so. We have also examined the hard coded DAC permission table for properties in `property_service.c`, as well as the hardcoded specialty properties like the `ctl.` family. In the next chapter, we look at how the tool chain builds and creates all the policy files we have been using.

12
Mastering the Tool Chain

So far, we have taken a deep dive into the code and policies that drive SE for Android technologies, but the build system and tools are often overlooked. Mastering the tool chain will help you improve your development practices. In this chapter, we will look at all the components of the SE for Android build and how they work. We will cover the following topics:

- Building specific targets
- The sepolicy `Android.mk` file
- Custom build policy configuration
- Build tools:

    ◦ `check_seapp`
    ◦ `insertkeys.py`
    ◦ `checkpolicy`
    ◦ `checkfc`
    ◦ `sepolicy-check`
    ◦ `sepolicy-analyze`

Building subcomponents – targets and projects

So far, we have run some magical commands such as `mm`, `mmm`, and `make bootimage` to actually build various portions of the SE for Android code. Google officially describes some of these tools in the documents at `https://source.android.com/source/building-running.html`, but most commands are not listed. Nonetheless, `http://elinux.org/Android_Build_System` has a write up that is more comprehensive.

In Google's "building and running" documentation, they describe the target as the device, which is ultimately what you lunch for. When building Android, the `lunch` command sets up environment variables for the `make` command you execute later. It sets up the build system to output the correct configuration for the target device. This concept of a target is *not* what will be discussed in this chapter. Instead, when `target` is mentioned herein, it means a specific `make` target. However, in the event of needing to mention the target device, the complete phrase "`target device`" will be used. While somewhat confusing, this terminology is standard and will be understood by engineers in the field.

We have issued `make` a few times, optionally providing a target as an argument and an option, for example the `-j16` option. Something like `make` or `make -j16` essentially builds all of Android. Optionally, you can specify a target or list of targets as command arguments. An example of this is when `boot.img` was built. The `boot.img` file can be built and rebuilt by specifying the `bootimage` target. The command we use for this purpose is `make bootimage`. It helps to expedite builds by rebuilding only the portions of the system that are needed. But what if you only need to rebuild a particular file? Perhaps, you only want to rebuild `sepolicy`. You can specify that as the target to build, as in `make sepolicy`. This leads to the question, "What about the other files such as `mac_permissions.xml`, `seapp_contexts`, and so on?" They can be built in the same way. The more intriguing question is, "How does one know what the target name is? Is it always the file output name?"

Android's build system is constructed on top of GNU `make` (`http://www.gnu.org/software/make/`). The core of the Android build system's makefiles system can be found in `build/core`, and the documentation can be found in the NDK (`https://developer.android.com/tools/sdk/ndk/index.html`). The major take away from that reading is that a typical `Android.mk` file defines something called `LOCAL_MODULE := mymodulename`, and something called `mymodulename` is built. The target names are defined by these `LOCAL_MODULE` statements. Let's look at the `Android.mk` for external sepolicy, and focus on the sepolicy portion of it, as there are other local modules or targets defined in that `Makefile`. The following is an example from Android 4.3:

```
include $(CLEAR_VARS)
LOCAL_MODULE := sepolicy
LOCAL_MODULE_CLASS := ETC
LOCAL_MODULE_TAGS := optional
LOCAL_MODULE_PATH := $(TARGET_ROOT_OUT)
...
```

One can find all the modules for within an `Android.mk` file by just looking for lines that begin with `LOCAL_MODULE` declarations and are whole word matches:

```
$ grep -w '^LOCAL_MODULE' Android.mk
LOCAL_MODULE := sepolicy
LOCAL_MODULE := file_contexts
LOCAL_MODULE := seapp_contexts
LOCAL_MODULE := property_contexts
LOCAL_MODULE := selinux-network.sh
LOCAL_MODULE := mac_permissions.xml
LOCAL_MODULE := eops.xml
```

Regular expressions dictate that ^ is the beginning of the line, and the `grep` man page states that `-w` provides whole word search.

The preceding list is comprehensive for the version of Android we are using on the UDOO. However, you should run the command on your exact version of the `Makefile` to get an idea of what things can be built.

Android has some additional tools that are separate from building targets and get added to your environment when you use `source build/envsetup.sh`. These are mm and mmm. They both perform the same task, which is to build all the targets specified in an `Android.mk` file, however, differing that they do not build any of their dependencies. The two commands only differ in where they source the location of the `Android.mk` to scour for build targets. The mm command uses the current working directory, whereas mmm uses a supplied path. Also, a great option for either command is `-B`, which forces a rebuild. An engineer can save a lot of time by using the mm(m) commands over `make <target>`. The full `make` command wastes a lot of time figuring out the dependency tree, so executing `mmm path/to/project` on a previously built source tree (if you know that all your changes are within a project) can save a few minutes. However, since it doesn't build the dependencies, you'll need to ensure that they are already built and have no dependent changes.

Exploring sepolicy's Android.mk

The project located at `external/sepolicy` uses an `Android.mk` file, like any other Android project, to build their outputs. Let's dissect this file and see what it does.

Building sepolicy

We'll start in the middle by looking at the target for `sepolicy`. It starts off with fairly boilerplate `Android.mk` stuff:

```
...
include $(CLEAR_VARS)
LOCAL_MODULE := sepolicy
LOCAL_MODULE_CLASS := ETC
LOCAL_MODULE_TAGS := optional
LOCAL_MODULE_PATH := $(TARGET_ROOT_OUT)
include $(BUILD_SYSTEM)/base_rules.mk
...
```

The next portion is a bit more like standard `make`. It starts off by declaring a target file that gets built into the `intermediates` location. The `intermediates` location is defined by the Android build system. It then assigns the values of `MLS_SENS` and `MLS_CATS` to some local variables for later use. The last line is the most interesting. It uses a `make` function, called `build_policy`, and takes filenames as arguments:

```
...
sepolicy_policy.conf := $(intermediates)/policy.conf
$(sepolicy_policy.conf): PRIVATE_MLS_SENS := $(MLS_SENS)
$(sepolicy_policy.conf): PRIVATE_MLS_CATS := $(MLS_CATS)
$(sepolicy_policy.conf) : $(call build_policy, security_classes
initial_sids access_vectors global_macros mls_macros mls policy_
capabilities te_macros attributes bools *.te roles users initial_sid_
contexts fs_use genfs_contexts port_contexts)
...
```

Next, we define the recipe for building this intermediate target, `policy.conf`. The interesting bits of the recipe are the `m4` command and the `sed` command.

> For more information on m4, see http://www.gnu.org/software/m4/manual/m4.html, and for more information on sed, refer to https://www.gnu.org/software/sed/manual/sed.html.

SELinux policy files get processed using m4. m4 is a macro processor language that is often used as a frontend to a compiler. The m4 command takes some of the values such as PRIVATE_MLS_SENS and PRIVATE_MLS_CATS and passes them through as macro definitions. This is analogous to the gcc -D option. It then takes the dependencies for the target as input via the make expansion, $^, and outputs them to the target name using the make expansion of $@. It also takes that output and generates a .dontaudit version. That version has all of the dontaudit lines deleted from the policy file using sed. The MLS values tell SELinux how many categories and sensitivities to generate. These must be statically defined in the policy blob that is loaded into the kernel, as follows:

```
. . .
@mkdir -p $(dir $@)
$(hide) m4 -D mls_num_sens=$(PRIVATE_MLS_SENS) -D mls_num_
cats=$(PRIVATE_MLS_CATS) -s $^ > $@
$(hide) sed '/dontaudit/d' $@ > $@.dontaudit
. . .
```

The next portion defines the recipe for building the actual target, named from LOCAL_MODULE_POLICY, even if this is not obvious. LOCAL_BUILT_MODULE expands to the intermediate file to be built, sepolicy in this case. It finally gets copied by the Android build system as LOCAL_INSTALLED_MODULE behind the scenes. This target depends on the intermediate policy.conf file and on checkpolicy. It uses checkpolicy to transform the m4 expanded policy.conf and policy.conf.dontaudit into two sepolicy files, sepolicy and sepolicy.dontaudit. The actual tool that is used to compile the SELinux statements in binary form to load to the kernel is checkpolicy, as follows:

```
. . .
$(LOCAL_BUILT_MODULE) : $(sepolicy_policy.conf) $(HOST_OUT_
EXECUTABLES)/checkpolicy
@mkdir -p $(dir $@)
$(hide) $(HOST_OUT_EXECUTABLES)/checkpolicy -M -c $(POLICYVERS) -o $@
$<
$(hide) $(HOST_OUT_EXECUTABLES)/checkpolicy -M -c $(POLICYVERS) -o
$(dir $<)/$(notdir $@).dontaudit $<.dontaudit
. . .
```

Finally, it ends by setting a local variable, built_policy, for use elsewhere within the Android.mk file, and clears policy.conf to avoid polluting the global namespace of make, as shown:

```
. . .
built_sepolicy := $(LOCAL_BUILT_MODULE)
sepolicy_policy.conf :=
. . .
```

Additionally, building `sepolicy` also depends on the `POLICYVERS` variable, which is conditionally assigned a value of `26` if not set. This is the policy version number used by `checkpolicy`, and as we saw earlier in the book, we had to override this for our UDOO.

Controlling the policy build

We saw that the `sepolicy` statement calls the `build_policy` function. We also see its use in that `Android.mk` file for building `sepolicy`, `file_contexts`, `seapp_contexts`, `property_contexts`, and `mac_permissions.xml`, so it reasons that it is fairly important. This function outputs a list of fully resolved paths used for policy files. The function takes as inputs a variable argument list of filenames and includes regular expression support (note `*.te` in the `build_policy` for target sepolicy). Internally, that function uses some magic to allow you to override or append to the current policy build without modifying the `external/sepolicy` directory directly. This is meant for OEMs and device builders to be able to augment policy to cover their specific devices.

When building a policy, you can set the following `make` variables, typically in the device's `Makefile`, to control the resulting build. The variables are as follows:

- `BOARD_SEPOLICY_DIRS`: This is the search path for potential policy files
- `BOARD_SEPOLICY_UNION`: This is a policy file of name to append to all files with the same name
- `BOARD_SEPOLICY_REPLACE`: This is a policy file used to override the base `external/sepolicy` policy file
- `BOARD_SEPOLICY_IGNORE`: This is used to remove a particular policy file from the build, given a repository's relative path

Using the UDOO as an example, the proper way to author a policy was never to modify `external/sepolicy` but to create a directory in `device/fsl/udoo/sepolicy`:

```
$ mkdir <PATH>
```

Then we modify the `BoardConfig.mk`:

```
$ vim BoardConfig.mk
```

Next, we add the following lines:

```
BOARD_SEPOLICY_DIRS += device/fsl/udoo/sepolicy
```

Be very careful with += as opposed to :=. In large project trees, some of these variables may be set higher in the build tree by common BoardConfigs, and you could wipe out their settings. Typically, the safest bet is +=. For further details, see *Variable Assignment* in the GNU make manual, at http://www.gnu.org/software/make/manual/make.html.

This will tell the build_policy() function in Android.mk to search not only external/sepolicy but also device/fsl/udoo/sepolicy for policy files.

Next, we can create a file_contexts file in this directory, and move our changes for labeling to this directory by creating a new file_contexts file in device/fsl/udoo/sepolicy.

After this, we need to instruct the build system to combine, or union, our file_contexts file with the one in external/sepolicy. We accomplish this by adding the following statement to the BoardConfig.mk file:

```
BOARD_SEPOLICY_UNION += file_contexts
```

You can do this for any policy file, even custom files. It does a match on the filename by basename only (no directories). For instance, if you had a watchdog.te rules file you wanted to add to the base watchdog.te rules file, you could just add watchdog.te, as shown:

```
BOARD_SEPOLICY_UNION += file_contexts watchdog.te
```

This produces a new watchdog.te file during the build that unions your new rules with the ones found in external/sepolicy/watchdog.te.

Also note that you add new files into the build with BOARD_SEPOLICY_UNION, so to add a .te file for a custom domain, such as custom.te, you could:

```
BOARD_SEPOLICY_UNION += file_contexts watchdog.te custom.te
```

Let's say you want to override the external/sepolicy watchdog.te file with your own. You can add it to BOARD_SEPOLICY_REPLACE, as shown:

```
BOARD_SEPOLICY_REPLACE := watchdog.te
```

Note that you can't replace a file that does not exist in the base policy. Also, you can't have the same file appear in UNION and REPLACE, as it's ambiguous. You can't have more than one specification of BOARD_SEPOLICY_REPLACE on the same policy file.

Suppose we have a hierarchical build occurring for two fictitious devices, device X and device Y. The two devices, device X and device Y, both inherit `BoardConfigCommon.mk` from device A. Device A is not a real device, but since X and Y share commonalities, the common bits are kept in device A.

Suppose the `BoardConfigCommon.mk` for device A contains these statements:

```
BOARD_SEPOLICY_DIRS += device/OEM/A
BOARD_SEPOLICY_UNION += file_contexts custom.te
```

Suppose that device X's `BoardConfig.mk` contains:

```
BOARD_SEPOLICY_DIRS += device/OEM/X
BOARD_SEPOLICY_UNION += file_contexts custom.te
```

Finally, suppose device Y's `BoardConfig.mk` contains:

```
BOARD_SEPOLICY_DIRS += device/OEM/Y
BOARD_SEPOLICY_UNION += file_contexts custom.te
```

The resulting policy sets used to build device X and device Y are the following:

Device X policy set:

```
device/OEM/A/file_contexts
device/OEM/A/custom.te
device/OEM/X/file_contexts
device/OEM/X/custome.te
external/sepolicy/* (base policy files)
```

Device Y also contains:

```
device/OEM/A/file_contexts
device/OEM/A/custom.te
device/OEM/Y/file_contexts
device/OEM/Y/custom.te
external/sepolicy/* (base policy files)
```

In a common scenario, you might not want the resulting policy set for device Y to contain `device/OEM/A/custom.te`. This is a use case for `BOARD_SEPOLICY_IGNORE`. You can use this to filter out specific policy files. However, you have to be specific and use the repository's relative path. For example, in device Y's `BoardConfig.mk`:

```
BOARD_SEPOLICY_IGNORE += device/OEM/A/custom.te
```

Now, when you build a policy for device Y, the policy set will not include that file. BOARD_SEPOLICY_IGNORE can also be used with BOARD_SEPOLICY_REPLACE, allowing multiple uses in the device hierarchy, but only one BOARD_SEPOLICY_REPLACE statement takes effect.

Digging deeper into build_policy

Now that we have seen how to use some new mechanisms to control the policy build, let's actually dissect where in the build process happens. As stated earlier, the policy build is controlled by the Android.mk file. We encountered calls to the build_policy() function earlier, and this is precisely where the magic happens with respect to all of the BOARD_SEPOLICY_* variables we set. Examining the build_ policy function, we see references to the sepolicy_replace_paths variable, so let's start by looking at that variable.

The sepolicy_replace_paths variable begins life by getting evaluated when the Makefile is evaluated. In other words, it is executed unconditionally. The code starts off by looping over all the BOARD_SEPOLICY_REPLACE files and checks whether any are in BOARD_SEPOLICY_UNION. If one is found, an error is printed and the build fails, showing Ambiguous request for sepolicy $(pf). Appears in both BOARD_ SEPOLICY_REPLACE and BOARD_SEPOLICY_UNION, where $(pf) is expanded to the offending policy file. After that, it expands the BOARD_SEPOLICY_REPLACE entries with those found on the search paths set by BOARD_SEPOLICY_DIRS, thus resulting in full relative paths from the root of the Android tree. Then it filters these entries against BOARD_SEPOLICY_IGNORE, dropping anything that should be ignored. It then ensures that only one file candidate for replacement is found. Otherwise, it issues the appropriate error message. Lastly, it ensures that the file exists in the LOCAL_PATH or base policy, and if none of the two is found, it issues an error message:

```
...
# Quick edge case error detection for BOARD_SEPOLICY_REPLACE.
# Builds the singular path for each replace file.
sepolicy_replace_paths :=
$(foreach pf, $(BOARD_SEPOLICY_REPLACE), \
  $(if $(filter $(pf), $(BOARD_SEPOLICY_UNION)), \
    $(error Ambiguous request for sepolicy $(pf). Appears in both \
      BOARD_SEPOLICY_REPLACE and BOARD_SEPOLICY_UNION), \
  ) \
  $(eval _paths := $(filter-out $(BOARD_SEPOLICY_IGNORE), \
  $(wildcard $(addsuffix /$(pf), $(BOARD_SEPOLICY_DIRS)))))) \
  $(eval _occurrences := $(words $(_paths))) \
  $(if $(filter 0,$(_occurrences)), \
    $(error No sepolicy file found for $(pf) in $(BOARD_SEPOLICY_
DIRS)), \
```

```
    ) \
  $(if $(filter 1, $(_occurrences)), \
    $(eval sepolicy_replace_paths += $(_paths)), \
    $(error Multiple occurrences of replace file $(pf) in $(_paths)) \
  ) \
  $(if $(filter 0, $(words $(wildcard $(addsuffix /$(pf), $(LOCAL_
PATH))))), \
    $(error Specified the sepolicy file $(pf) in BOARD_SEPOLICY_
REPLACE, \
      but none found in $(LOCAL_PATH)), \
  ) \
)
```

After this, calls to build policy can use `replace_paths` as an expanded list of files that will be replaced during the build.

The arguments of the `build_policy` function are the filenames you wish to expand into their Android root-relative path names, using the power provided by the `BOARD_SEPOLICY_*` family of variables. For instance, a call to `$(build_policy, file_contexts)` in the context of our devices A, X, and Y would result in this:

```
device/OEM/A/file_contexts
device/OEM/Y/file_contexts
```

The `build_policy` function is a bit tricky to read. Many nested function calls result in the deepest indents running first. However, like all code, we read it from top to bottom left to right, so the explanation will begin there. The function starts by looping through all the files passed as arguments. It then expands them against the `BOARD_SEPOLICY_DIRS` once for replace and once for a union. The `sepolicy_replace_paths` variable is error checked to ensure a file does not appear in both locations, replace and union. For the replace path expansion, it checks whether the expanded path is in `sepolicy_replace_dirs`, and if it is, replaces it. For the union portion, it just expands them. The results of these expansions are then fed through a filter on `BOARD_SEPOLICY_IGNORE`, thus dropping any of the explicitly ignored paths:

```
# Builds paths for all requested policy files w.r.t
# both BOARD_SEPOLICY_REPLACE and BOARD_SEPOLICY_UNION
# product variables.
# $(1): the set of policy name paths to build
build_policy = $(foreach type, $(1), \
  $(filter-out $(BOARD_SEPOLICY_IGNORE), \
    $(foreach expanded_type, $(notdir $(wildcard $(addsuffix /$(type),
$(LOCAL_PATH)))), \
      $(if $(filter $(expanded_type), $(BOARD_SEPOLICY_REPLACE)), \
        $(wildcard $(addsuffix $(expanded_type), $(sort $(dir
$(sepolicy_replace_paths)))))), \
```

```
        $(LOCAL_PATH)/$(expanded_type) \
    ) \
  ) \
    $(foreach union_policy, $(wildcard $(addsuffix /$(type), $(BOARD_
SEPOLICY_DIRS))), \
      $(if $(filter $(notdir $(union_policy)), $(BOARD_SEPOLICY_
UNION)), \
        $(union_policy), \
      ) \
    ) \
  ) \
)
...
```

Building mac_permissions.xml

The mac_permissions.xml build is a bit tricky, as we saw in *Chapter 10*, *Placing Applications in Domains*. First, mac_permissions.xml can be used with all the BOARD_SEPOLICY_* variables introduced thus far. The end result is one XML file adhering to the rules of those variables. Additionally, the raw XML files are processed by a tool called insertkeys.py, located in sepolicy/tools. The insertkeys.py tool uses keys.conf to map tags in the XML file signature stanza with .pem files containing the certificate. The keys.conf file is also subject to use in BOARD_SEPOLICY_* variables. The build recipe first calls build_policy on keys.conf and uses m4 to concatenate the results. Thus, m4 declarations in keys.conf will be respected. However, this has not been used. The initial intention was to use the m4 -s sync lines so that you can follow the inclusion chain in the keys.conf file when concatenated by m4 processing. On the other hand, sync lines are provided by m4 when concatenating many files, and they provide commented lines adhering to the #line NUM "FILE"' lines. These are useful because m4 takes multiple input files and combines them into a single, expanded output file. There will be sync lines indicating the beginning of each of those files, and they can help you track down issues. Continuing back to the mac_permissions.xml build, after expansion of keys.conf by m4, this file, along with all the mac_permissions.xml files from a call to build_policy() are finally fed to insertkeys.py. The insertkeys.py tool then uses the keys.conf file to replace all matching signature=<TAG> lines with an actual hex-encoded X509 from the PEM file, that is, signature=308E3600. Additionally, the insertkeys.py tool combines the XML files into one file, and strips whitespace and comments to reduce its size on disk. This has no build dependencies on the other major files such as sepolicy, seapp_contexts, property_contexts, and mac_permissions.xml.

Building seapp_contexts

The seapp_contexts file is also subject to all the BOARD_SEPOLICY_* variables. All of the seapp_contexts files from a resultant call to build_policy() are also fed through m4 -s to get a single seapp_contexts file that contains sync lines. Again, like mac_permissions.xml file's build of keys.conf, m4 hasn't been used other than for the synclines. This resulting, concatenated seapp_contexts file is then fed into check_seapp. This tool is authored in the C programming language and built into an executable during the build. The source can be found in tools/check_seapp. This tool reads the seapp_contexts file and checks its syntax. It verifies that there are no invalid key value pairs, that levelFrom is a valid identifier, and that the type and domain fields are valid for a given sepolicy. This build is dependent on sepolicy for the strict type checking of domain and type fields against the policy file.

Building file_contexts

The file_contexts file is also subject to all of the BOARD_SEPOLICY_* variables. The resulting set is passed through m4 -s, and the single output is run through the checkfc tool. The checkfc tool checks the grammar and syntax of the file and also verifies that the types exist in the built sepolicy. Because of this, it is dependent on the sepolicy build.

Building property_contexts

The property_contexts behaves exactly like the file_contexts build, except that it checks a property_contexts file. It also uses checkfc.

Current NSA research files

Additionally, work on Enterprise Operations (eops) is already underway at the NSA. As this feature hasn't been merged into mainstream Android and is likely to change wildly, it won't be covered here. However, the best place for the bleeding edge is always the source and NSA Bitbucket repositories. The selinux-network. sh also falls under this category; it hasn't seen mainstream adoption yet, and will likely be dropped from AOSP (https://android-review.googlesource. com/#/c/114380/).

Standalone tools

There are also some standalone tools built for Android policy evaluation that you may find useful. We will explore some of them and their usages. Most of the standard desktop tools you'll find in other references still work on SE for Android SELinux policy. Note that if you run any of the following tools and get a segmentation fault, you will likely need to apply the patch from the thread at http://marc.info/?l=seandroid-list&m=141684060409894&w=2.

sepolicy-check

This tool allows you to see whether a given allow rule exists in a policy file. The basic syntax of its command is as follows:

```
sepolicy-check -s <domain> -t <type> -c <class> -p <permission> -P
<policy_file>
```

For instance, if you want to see whether system_app can write to system_data_file for class file, you can execute:

```
$ sepolicy-check -s system_app -t system_data_file -c file -p write -P
$OUT/root/sepolicy
```

sepolicy-analyze

This is a good tool to check for common issues in SELinux development and it catches some of the common pitfalls of new SELinux policy writers. It can check for equivalent domains, duplicate allow rules. It can also perform policy type difference checks.

The domain equivalence check feature is very helpful. It shows you domains you may (in theory) want to be different, even though they converged in the implementation. These types would be ideal candidates to coalesce. However, it might have also shown an issue in the design of the policy that should be corrected. In other words, you didn't expect these domains to be equivalent. Invoking the command is as follows:

```
$ sepolicy-analyze -e -P $OUT/root/sepolicy
```

The duplicate allow rule checks whether allow rules exist on types that also exist on attributes that the type inherits from. The allow rule on the specific type is a candidate for removal, since there is already an allow on the attribute. To execute this check, run the following command:

```
$sepolicy-analyze -D -P $OUT/root/sepolicy
```

The difference is also handy is also handy to view type differences within a file. If you want to see what the difference between two domains is, you can use this feature. This is useful for identifying possible domains to coalesce. To perform this check, execute the following command:

```
$sepolicy-analyze -d -P $OUT/root/sepolicy
```

Summary

In this chapter, we covered how the various components that control the policy on the device are actually built and created, such as `sepolicy` and `mac_permissions`. `xml`. This chapter also presented the `BOARD_SEPOLICY_*` variables used to manage and build a policy across devices and configurations. Then we reviewed the `Android.mk` components, detailing how the heart of the build and configuration management works.

13
Getting to Enforcing Mode

As an engineer, you're handed some Android device, and the requirement is to apply SE for Android controls to the device to enhance its security posture. So far, we have seen all the pieces that need to be configured and how they work to enable such a system. In this chapter, we'll take all the skills covered to get our UDOO in enforcing mode. We will:

- Run, evaluate, and respond to audit logs from CTS
- Develop secure policy for the UDOO
- Switch to enforcing mode

Updating to SEPolicy master

Many changes to the `sepolicy` directory have occurred in the AOSP `master` branch since the 4.3 release. At the time of this writing, the `master` branch of the `external/sepolicy` project was on Git commit SHA `b5ffb`. The authors recommend attempting to use the most recent commit. However, for illustrative purposes, we will show you how to optionally check out commit `b5ffb` so you can accurately follow the examples in this chapter.

First, you'll need to clone the `external/sepolicy` project. In these instructions, we assume your working directory has the UDOO sources contained in the `./udoo` directory:

```
$ git clone https://android.googlesource.com/platform/external/sepolicy
$ cd sepolicy
```

If you want to follow the examples in this chapter precisely, you'll need to check out commit `b5ffb` with the following command. If you skip it, you will end up using the latest commit in the `master` branch:

```
$ git checkout b5ffb
```

Now, we'll replace the UDOO 4.3 sepolicy with what we just acquired from Google:

```
$ cd ..
$ rm -rf udoo/external/sepolicy
$ cp -r sepolicy udoo/external/sepolicy
```

Optionally, you can remove the `.git` folder from the newly copied sepolicy with the following command, but this is not necessary:

```
$ rm -rf udoo/external/sepolicy/.git
```

Also, copy the `audit.te` file and restore it.

Additionally, restore the `auditd` commit from the NSA Bitbucket `seandroid` repository. For your reference, it's commit SHA `d270aa3`.

After that, remove all references to `setool` from `udoo/build/core/Makefile`. This command will help you locate them:

```
$ grep -nw setool udoo/build/core/Makefile
```

Purging the device

At this point, our UDOO is messy, so let's reflash it, including the data directory, and start afresh. We want to have only the code and the `init` script changes, without the additional sepolicy. Then we can author a policy properly and apply all the techniques and tools we've encountered. We'll start by resetting to a state analogous to the completion of *Chapter 4, Installation on the UDOO*. However, the major difference is we need to build a `userdebug` version rather than an engineering (`eng`) version for CTS. The version is selected in the setup script, which ultimately calls `lunch`. To build this version, execute the following commands from the UDOO workspace:

```
$ . setup udoo-userdebug
$ make -j8 2>&1 | tee logz
```

Flash the system, boot to the SD card, and wipe `userdata` with the following commands, assuming the SD card is inserted into the host and `userdata` is not mounted:

```
$ mkdir ~/userdata
$ sudo mount /dev/sdd4 ~/userdata
$ cd ~/userdata/
$ sudo rm -rf *
$ cd ..
$ sudo umount ~/userdata
```

Setting up CTS

You must pass CTS if your organization seeks Android branding. However, even if you don't, it's a good idea to run these tests to help ensure a device will be compliant with applications. Based on your security goals and desires, you may fail portions of CTS if you're not seeking Android branding. For our case, we're looking at CTS as a way to exercise the system and uncover policy issues that prevent the proper functioning of the UDOO. Its source is located in the `cts/` directory, but we recommend downloading the binary directly from Google. You can get more information and the CTS binary itself from `https://source.android.com/compatibility/cts-intro.html` and `https://source.android.com/compatibility/android-cts-manual.pdf`.

Download the CTS 4.3 binary from the **Downloads** tab. Then select the CTS binary. The **Compatibility Definition Document** (**CDD**) is also worth reading. It covers the high-level details of CTS and compatibility requirements.

Download CTS from `https://source.android.com/compatibility/downloads.html` and extract it. Select the CTS version that matches your Android version. If you don't know which version your device is running, you can always check the `ro.build.version.release` property from the UDOO with `getprop ro.build.version.release`:

```
$ mkdir ~/udoo-cts
$ cd ~/udoo-cts
$ wget https://dl.google.com/dl/android/cts/android-cts-4.3_r2-linux_x86-arm.zip
$ unzip android-cts-4.3_r2-linux_x86-arm.zip
```

Running CTS

The CTS exercises many components on the device and helps test various parts of the system. A good, general policy should allow proper functioning of Android and pass CTS.

Follow the directions in the Android CTS user manual to set up your device (see *Section 3.3, Setting up your device*). Typically, you will see some failures if you don't follow all the steps precisely, as you may not have the access or the capabilities to acquire all the resources needed. However, CTS will still exercise some code paths. At a minimum, we recommend getting the media files copied and Wi-Fi active. Once your device is set up, ensure `adb` is active and initiate the testing:

```
$ ./cts-tradefed
11-30 10:30:08 I/: Detected new device 0123456789ABCDEF
```

```
cts-tf > run cts --plan CTS

cts-tf >

time passes here

11-30 10:30:28 I/TestInvocation: Starting invocation for 'cts' on build
'4.3_r2' on device 0123456789ABCDEF

11-30 10:30:28 I/0123456789ABCDEF: Created result dir 2014.11.30_10.30.28

11-30 10:31:44 I/0123456789ABCDEF: Collecting device info

11-30 10:31:45 I/0123456789ABCDEF: ------------------------------------
---

11-30 10:31:45 I/0123456789ABCDEF: Test package android.aadb started

11-30 10:31:45 I/0123456789ABCDEF: ------------------------------------
---

11-30 10:32:15 I/0123456789ABCDEF: com.android.cts.aadb.TestDeviceFuncTes
t#testBugreport PASS

...
```

The tests take many hours to execute, so be patient; but you can check the status of
the test:

```
cts-tf > l i

Command Id  Exec Time Device State

1 8m:22 0123456789ABCDEF running cts on build 4.3_r2
```

Plug in speakers to enjoy the sounds from the media tests and ringtones! Also, CTS
reboots the device. If your ADB session is not restored after rebooting, ADB may not
execute any tests. Use the `--disable-reboot` option when running the `cts-tf >
run cts --plan CTS --disable-reboot` plan.

Gathering the results

First, we'll consider the CTS results. Although we expect some failures, we also
expect the problem will not get worse when we go to enforcing mode. Second,
we'll look at the audit logs. Let's pull both of these files from the device.

CTS test results

CTS creates a test results directory each time it is run. CTS is indicating the directory
name but not the location:

```
11-30 10:30:28 I/0123456789ABCDEF: Created result dir 2014.11.30_10.30.28
```

The location is mentioned by the CTS manual and can be found under the extracted CTS directory in `repository/results`, typically at `android-cts/repository/results`. The test directories contain an XML test report, `testResult.xml`. This can be opened in most web browsers. It has a nice overview of the tests and details of all executed tests. The `pass:fail` ratio is our baseline. The authors had 18,736 pass, and only 53 fail, which is fairly good considering half of those are feature issues, such as no Bluetooth or returning true for camera support.

Audit logs

We will use the audit logs to address deficiencies in our policy. Pull these off the device using the standard `adb pull` commands we have used throughout the book. Since this is a `userdebug` build and default `adb` terminals are shell `uid` (not root), start `adb` as root with `adb root`. `su` is also available on `userdebug` builds.

> You may get an error saying `/data/misc/audit/audit.log` does not exist. The solution is to run `adb` as root via the `adb root` command. Also, when running this command, it may hang. Just go to settings, disable, and then enable **USB Debugging** under **Developer Options**. Then kill the `adb-root` command and verify you have root by running `adb shell`. Now you should be a root user again.

Authoring device policy

Run both `audit.log` and `audit.old` through `audit2allow` to see what's going on. The output of `audit2allow` is grouped by source domain. Rather than going through it all, we will highlight the unusual cases, starting with the interpreted results of `audit2allow`. Assuming you are in the audit log directory, perform `cat audit.* | audit2allow | less`. Any policy work will be done in the device-specific UDOO sepolicy directory.

adbd

The following are our `adbd` denials as filtered through `audit2allow`:

```
#============== adbd ==============
allow adbd ashmem_device:chr_file execute;
allow adbd dumpstate:unix_stream_socket connectto;
allow adbd dumpstate_socket:sock_file write;
allow adbd input_device:chr_file { write getattr open };
allow adbd log_device:chr_file { write read ioctl open };
```

```
allow adbd logcat_exec:file { read getattr open execute execute_no_
trans };
allow adbd mediaserver:binder { transfer call };
allow adbd mediaserver:fd use;
allow adbd self:capability { net_raw dac_override };
allow adbd self:process execmem;
allow adbd shell_data_file:file { execute execute_no_trans };
allow adbd system_server:binder { transfer call };
allow adbd tmpfs:file execute;
allow adbd unlabeled:dir getattr;
```

The denials in the `adbd` domain are quite strange. The first thing that caught our eye was the `execute` on `/dev/ashmem`, which is a character driver. Typically, this is only needed for Dalvik JIT. Looking at the raw audits (`cat audit.* | grep adbd | grep execute`), we see the following:

```
type=1400 msg=audit(1417416666.182:788): avc: denied { execute } for
pid=3680 comm="Compiler" path=2F6465762F6173686D656D2F64616C76696B2D
6A69742D636F646520286465C6574656429 dev=tmpfs ino=412027
scontext=u:r:adbd:s0 tcontext=u:object_r:tmpfs:s0 tclass=file

type=1400 msg=audit(1417416670.352:831): avc: denied { execute }
for pid=3753 comm="Compiler" path="/dev/ashmem" dev=tmpfs ino=1127
scontext=u:r:adbd:s0 tcontext=u:object_r:ashmem_device:s0 tclass=chr_file
```

Something with the process `comm` field of the compiler is executing on `ashmem`. Our guess is it has something to do with Dalvik, but why is it in the `adbd` domain? Also, why is `adbd` writing to the input device? All this is strange behavior. Typically, when you see things like this, it's because the children didn't end up in the proper domain. Run this command to check the domains and confirm our suspicions:

```
$ adb shell ps -Z | grep adbd
u:r:adbd:s0 root 20046 1 /sbin/adbd
u:r:adbd:s0 root 20101 20046 ps
```

We then run `adb shell ps -Z | grep adbd` to see which things were running in the `adb` domain, further confirming our suspicions:

```
u:r:adbd:s0 root 20046 1 /sbin/adbd
u:r:adbd:s0 root 20101 20046 ps
```

The `ps` command should not be running in the `adbd` context; it should be running in `shell`. This confirmed that `shell` is not in the right domain:

```
$ adb shell
root@udoo:/ # id
uid=0(root) gid=0(root) context=u:r:adbd:s0
```

The first thing to check is the context on the file:

```
root@udoo:/ # ls -Z /system/bin/sh
lrwxr-xr-x root shell u:object_r:system_file:s0 sh -> mksh
root@udoo:/ # ls -Z /system/bin/mksh
-rwxr-xr-x root shell u:object_r:system_file:s0 mksh
```

The base policy defines a domain transition when `adbd` loads the shell using `exec` to go to the shell domain. This is defined in the `adbd.te` external sepolicy as `domain_auto_trans(adbd, shell_exec, shell)`.

Obviously, an incorrect label has been applied to shell, so let's look at `file_contexts` in the external sepolicy to find out why.

```
$ cat file_contexts | grep shell_exec
/system/bin/sh -- u:object_r:shell_exec:s0
```

The two dashes mean that only regular files will be labeled and symbolic links will be skipped. We probably don't want to label the symlink, but rather the `mksh` destination. Do this by adding a custom `file_contexts` entry to the device UDOO sepolicy and adding the file to the `BOARD_SEPOLICY_UNION` config. In `file_contexts`, add `/system/bin/mksh -- u:object_r:shell_exec:s0`, and in `sepolicy.mk`, add `BOARD_SEPOLICY_UNION += file_contexts`.

 Throughout the remainder of the chapter, whenever you create or modify policy files (for example, context files or `*.te` files), don't forget to add them to `BOARD_SEPOLICY_UNION` in `sepolicy.mk`.

Since this is a fairly fatal issue with the policy and `adbd`, we won't worry about the denials for now, with the exception of the unlabeled. Whenever one encounters an unlabeled file, it should be addressed. The `avc` denial that caused this is as follows:

```
type=1400 msg=audit(1417405835.872:435): avc: denied { getattr
} for pid=4078 comm="ls" path="/device" dev=mmcblk0p7 ino=2
scontext=u:r:adbd:s0 tcontext=u:object_r:unlabeled:s0 tclass=dir
```

Because this is mounted at `/device` and Android mounts are typically at `/`, we should look at the mount table:

```
root@udoo:/ # mount | grep device
/dev/block/mmcblk0p7 /device ext4 ro,seclabel,nosuid,nodev,relatime,us
er_xattr,barrier=1,data=ordered 0 0
```

Typically, mount commands are in the init scripts following a `mkdir`, or in an `fstab` file with the init built-in, `mount_all`. A quick search for `device` and `mkdir` in `init.rc` finds nothing, but we do find it in `fstab.freescale`. The device is read-only, so we should be able to give it a type, label it with file contexts, and apply the `getattr` domain to its directory class. Since it's read-only and empty, nobody should need more permissions. Looking at the `make_sd.sh` script, we notice that partition 7 of the block device is the `vender` directory. This is a misspelling of the common vendor directory that OEMs place proprietary blobs in. We place file types in `file.te` and the domain allow rules in `domain.te`.

In `file.te`, add this:

```
type udoo_device_file, file_type;
```

In `domain.te`, add the following:

```
allow domain udoo_device_file:dir getattr;
```

In `file_contexts`, add this:

```
/device u:object_r:udoo_device_file:s0
```

If this directory is not empty, you must manually run `restorecon -R` on it to label existing files.

If you pull the audit logs multiple times from the UDOO, you may also end up with denials showing that you did so, as `adbd` will not be able to access them. You may see this:

```
#============= adbd ==============
allow adbd audit_log:file { read getattr open };
```

This rule comes from the end of the test when you `adb pulled` the audit logs. We can safely `dontaudit` this and add a `neverallow` to ensure it doesn't accidentally get allowed. The audit logs contain information a malware writer could use to navigate through the policy, and this information should be protected. In a device sepolicy folder, add an `adbd.te` file and union it in the `sepolicy.mk` file:

In `adbd.te`, add this:

```
# dont audit adb pull and adb shell cat of audit logs
dontaudit adbd audit_log:file r_file_perms;
dontaudit shell audit_log:file r_file_perms;
```

In `auditd.te`, add this:

```
# Make sure no one adds an allow to the audit logs
# from anything but system server (read only) and
# auditd, rw access.
neverallow { domain -system_server -auditd -init -kernel } audit_
log:file ~getattr;
neverallow system_server audit_log:file ~r_file_perms;
```

If `auditd.te` is still in `external/sepolicy`, move it to `device/fsl/udoo/sepolicy` along with all dependent types.

The `neverallow` entries show you how to use the compliment, ~, and set difference, -, operators for strong assertions or brevity. The first `neverallow` starts with domain, and all process types (domains) are members of the domain attribute. We prevent access through set difference, leaving the set that must never have access. We then compliment the access vector set to allow only `getattr` or `stat` on the logs. The second `neverallow` uses compliment to ensure `system_server` is limited to read operations.

bootanim

The `bootanim` domain is assigned to the boot animation service that presents splash screens on boot, typically the carrier's branding:

```
#============= bootanim ==============
allow bootanim init:unix_stream_socket connectto;
allow bootanim log_device:chr_file { write open };
allow bootanim property_socket:sock_file write;
```

Anything touching the `init` domain is a red flag. Here, `bootanim` connects to an init Unix domain socket. This is a part of the property system, and we can see that after connecting, it writes to the property socket. The socket object and its URI are separate. In this case, it's the filesystem, but it could be an anonymous socket:

```
type=1400 msg=audit(1417405616.640:255): avc: denied { connectto }
for pid=2534 comm="BootAnimation" path="/dev/socket/property_service"
scontext=u:r:bootanim:s0 tcontext=u:r:init:s0 tclass=unix_stream_socket
```

The `log_device` is deprecated in new versions of Android and replaced with `logd`. However, we are backporting a new master sepolicy to 4.3, so we must support this. The patch that removed support is at `https://android-review.googlesource.com/#/c/108147/`.

Rather than apply a reverse patch to the external sepolicy, we can just add the rules to our device policy in a `domain.te` file. We can safely allow these using the proper macros and styles in the device UDOO `sepolicy` folder. In `bootanim.te`, add `unix_socket_connect(bootanim, property, init)`, and in `domain.te`, add this:

```
allow domain udoo_device_file:dir getattr;
allow domain log_device:dir search;
allow domain log_device:chr_file rw_file_perms;
```

debuggerd

```
#============= debuggerd ==============
allow debuggerd log_device:chr_file { write read open };
allow debuggerd system_data_file:sock_file write;
```

The log device denial was addressed under `bootanim` by adding the allow rules for all domains to use `log_device`. The `system_data_file:sock_file write` is strange. In most circumstances, you'll almost never want to allow a cross-domain write, but this is special. Look at the raw denial:

```
type=1400 msg=audit(1417415122.602:502): avc: denied { write } for
pid=2284 comm="debuggerd" name="ndebugsocket" dev=mmcblk0p4 ino=129525
scontext=u:r:debuggerd:s0 tcontext=u:object_r:system_data_file:s0
tclass=sock_file
```

The denial is on `ndebugsocket`. Grepping for this uncovers a named type transition, which policy version 23 does not support:

```
system_server.te:297:type_transition system_server system_data_file:sock_
file system_ndebug_socket "ndebugsocket";
```

We have to change the code to set the proper context or just allow it, which we will. We won't grant additional permissions because it never asked for open, and we're crossing domains. Preventing file opens across domains is ideal, as the only way to get this file descriptor is through an IPC call into the owning domain. In `debuggerd.te`, add `allow debuggerd system_data_file:sock_file write;`.

drmserver

```
#============= drmserver ==============
allow drmserver log_device:chr_file { write open };
```

This is taken care of by `domain.te` rules, so we have nothing to do here.

dumpstate

```
#============= dumpstate ==============
allow dumpstate init:binder call;
allow dumpstate init:process signal;
allow dumpstate log_device:chr_file { write read open };
allow dumpstate node:rawip_socket node_bind;
allow dumpstate self:capability sys_resource;
allow dumpstate system_data_file:file { write rename create setattr };
```

The denial to init:binder call on dumpstate is strange because init doesn't use binder. Some process must stay in the init domain. Let's check our process listing for init:

```
$ adb shell ps -Z | grep init
u:r:init:s0 root 1 0 /init
u:r:init:s0 root 2286 1 zygote
u:r:init:s0 radio 2759 2286 com.android.phone
```

Here, zygote and com.android.phone should not be running as init. This must be a labeling error on the app_process file, which is the zygote. The ls -laZ / system/bin/app_process command reveals u:object_r:system_file:s0 app_process, so add an entry to file_contexts to correct this. We can find the label to use in zygote.te in the base sepolicy defined as the zygote_exec type:

```
# zygote
type zygote, domain;
type zygote_exec, exec_type, file_type;
```

In file_contexts, add /system/bin/app_process u:object_r:zygote_exec:s0.

installd

The added domain.te rules handle installd.

keystore

```
#============= keystore ==============
allow keystore app_data_file:file write;
allow keystore log_device:chr_file { write open };
```

The log device is taken care of by the `domain.te` rules. Let's look at the raw `app_data_file` denial:

```
type=1400 msg=audit(1417417454.442:845): avc: denied { write } for
pid=15339 comm="onCtsTestRunner" path="/data/data/com.android.cts.
stub/cache/CTS_DUMP" dev=mmcblk0p4 ino=131242 scontext=u:r:keystore:s0
tcontext=u:object_r:app_data_file:s0:c512,c768 tclass=file
```

Categories are defined in the contexts. This means MLS support is activated for app domains. In the `seapp_contexts` base sepolicy, we see this:

```
user=_app domain=untrusted_app type=app_data_file levelFrom=user
user=_app seinfo=platform domain=platform_app type=app_data_file
levelFrom=user
```

MLS separation of application data is still under development and didn't work on 4.3, so we can disable this. We can just declare them in a device-specific `seapp_contexts` file. In `seapp_contexts`, add `user=_app domain=untrusted_app type=app_data_file` and `user=_app seinfo=platform domain=platform_app type=app_data_file`. In 4.3, any changes to context on data require a factory reset. The 4.4 version added smart relabel capabilities.

mediaserver

```
#============== mediaserver ==============
allow mediaserver adbd:binder { transfer call };
allow mediaserver init:binder { transfer call };
allow mediaserver log_device:chr_file { write open };
```

The log device was addressed in the `domain.te` rules. We'll skip `init` and `adbd` too, since their issues were triggered by improper process domains. It's important not to add allow rules blindly, as most of the work for existing domains can be handled with small label changes or a few rules.

netd

```
#============== netd ==============
allow netd kernel:system module_request;
allow netd log_device:chr_file { write open };
```

The log device denial of netd was addressed by domain.te. However, we should scrutinize anything requesting a capability. When granting capabilities, the policy author needs to be very careful. If a domain is granted the ability to load a system module and that domain or module binary itself is compromised, it could lead to the injection of malware into the kernel via loadable modules. However, netd needs loadable kernel module support to support some cards. Add the allow rule to a file called netd.te in the device UDOO sepolicy. In netd.te, add allow netd self:capability sys_module;.

rild

```
#============= rild ==============
allow rild log_device:chr_file { write open };
```

This is taken care of by domain.te rules, so we have nothing to do here.

servicemanager

```
#============= servicemanager ==============
allow servicemanager init:binder transfer;
allow servicemanager log_device:chr_file { write open };
```

Again, the log device was handled in domain.te. We'll skip init, since its issues were triggered by improper process domains.

surfaceflinger

```
#============= surfaceflinger ==============
allow surfaceflinger init:binder transfer;
allow surfaceflinger log_device:chr_file { write open };
```

Again, the log device was handled in domain.te. We'll skip init too, since its issues were triggered by improper process domains.

system_server

```
#============= system_server ==============
allow system_server adbd:binder { transfer call };
allow system_server dalvikcache_data_file:file { write setattr };
allow system_server init:binder { transfer call };
allow system_server init:file write;
allow system_server init:process { setsched sigkill getsched };
allow system_server init_tmpfs:file read;
allow system_server log_device:chr_file write;
```

Since `log_device` is taken care of by `domain.te`, and `init` and `adbd` are polluted, we will only address the Dalvik cache denial:

```
type=1400 msg=audit(1417405611.550:159): avc: denied { write } for
pid=2571 comm="er.ServerThread" name="system@app@SettingsProvider.apk@
classes.dex" dev=mmcblk0p4 ino=129458 scontext=u:r:system_server:s0
tcontext=u:object_r:dalvikcache_data_file:s0 tclass=file

type=1400 msg=audit(1417405611.550:160): avc: denied { setattr } for
pid=2571 comm="er.ServerThread" name="system@app@SettingsProvider.apk@
classes.dex" dev=mmcblk0p4 ino=129458 scontext=u:r:system_server:s0
tcontext=u:object_r:dalvikcache_data_file:s0 tclass=file
```

The external sepolicy seandroid-4.3 branch allowed `domain.te:allow domain dalvikcache_data_file:file r_file_perms;`. Writes were allowed by `system_app` with `system_app.te:allow system_app dalvikcache_data_file:file { write setattr };`. We should be able to grant this write access because there may be a need to update its Dalvik cache file. In `domain.te`, add `allow domain dalvikcache_data_file:file r_file_perms;`, and in `system_server.te`, add `allow system_server dalvikcache_data_file:file { write setattr };`.

toolbox

```
#============= toolbox =============
allow toolbox sysfs:file write;
```

Typically, one should not write to `sysfs`. Now look at the raw denial for the offending `sysfs` file:

```
type=1400 msg=audit(1417405599.660:43): avc: denied { write
} for pid=2309 comm="cat" path="/sys/module/usbtouchscreen/
parameters/calibration" dev=sysfs ino=2318 scontext=u:r:toolbox:s0
tcontext=u:object_r:sysfs:s0 tclass=file
```

From here, we properly label `/sys/module/usbtouchscreen/parameters/calibration`. We place an entry in `file_contexts` to label `sysfs`, declare a type in `file.te`, and allow `toolbox` access to it. In `file.te`, add `type sysfs_touchscreen_calibration, fs_type, sysfs_type, mlstrustedobject;`, and in `file_contexts`, add `/sys/module/usbtouchscreen/parameters/calibration -- u:object_r:sysfs_touchscreen_calibration:s0`, and in `toolbox.te`, add `allow toolbox sysfs_touchscreen_calibration:file w_file_perms;`.

untrusted_app

```
#============= untrusted_app ==============
allow untrusted_app adb_device:chr_file getattr;
allow untrusted_app adbd:binder { transfer call };
allow untrusted_app adbd:dir { read getattr open search };
allow untrusted_app adbd:file { read getattr open };
allow untrusted_app adbd:lnk_file read;
...
```

untrusted_app had many denials. Considering the domain labeling issues, we won't address most of these now. However, you should look out for mislabeled and unlabeled target files. While searching the denial logs as interpreted by audit2allow, the following was found:

```
allow untrusted_app device:chr_file { read getattr };
allow untrusted_app unlabeled:dir { read getattr open };
```

For the chr_file device, we get this:

type=1400 msg=audit(1417416653.742:620): avc: denied { read } for pid=3696 comm="onCtsTestRunner" name="rfkill" dev=tmpfs ino=1126 scontext=u:r:untrusted_app:s0:c512,c768 tcontext=u:object_r:device:s0 tclass=chr_file

type=1400 msg=audit(1417416666.152:784): avc: denied { getattr } for pid=3696 comm="onCtsTestRunner" path="/dev/mxs_viim" dev=tmpfs ino=1131 scontext=u:r:untrusted_app:s0:c512,c768 tcontext=u:object_r:device:s0 tclass=chr_file

type=1400 msg=audit(1417416653.592:561): avc: denied { getattr } for pid=3696 comm="onCtsTestRunner" path="/dev/.coldboot_ done" dev=tmpfs ino=578 scontext=u:r:untrusted_app:s0:c512,c768 tcontext=u:object_r:device:s0 tclass=file

Therefore, we need to label /dev/.coldboot_done, /dev/rfkill properly, and /dev/mxs_viim. /dev/rfkill should be labeled in line with what the 4.3 policy had:

```
file_contexts:/sys/class/rfkill/rfkill[0-9]*/state --
u:object_r:sysfs_bluetooth_writable:s0
file_contexts:/sys/class/rfkill/rfkill[0-9]*/type -- u:object_r:sysfs_
bluetooth_writable:s0
```

The `/dev/mxs_viim` device seems to be a globally accessible GPU. We recommend a thorough review of the source code, but for now, we will label it as `gpu_device`. `/dev/.coldboot_done` is created by `ueventd` when the `coldboot` process completes. If `ueventd` is restarted, it skips the coldboot. We don't need to label this. This denial is caused by the source domain MLS on a target file that is not a subset of the categories of the source and does not have the `mlstrustedsubject` attribute; it should go away when we drop MLS support from apps.

In `file_contexts`:

```
# touch screen calibration
/sys/module/usbtouchscreen/parameters/calibration -- u:object_r:sysfs_
touchscreen_calibration:s0
#BT RFKill node
/sys/class/rfkill/rfkill[0-9]*/state -- u:object_r:sysfs_bluetooth_
writable:s0
/sys/class/rfkill/rfkill[0-9]*/type -- u:object_r:sysfs_bluetooth_
writable:s0
```

vold

```
#============= vold ==============
allow vold log_device:chr_file { write open };
```

Again, the log device was handled in `domain.te`.

watchdogd

```
#============= watchdogd ==============
allow watchdogd device:chr_file { read write create unlink open };
```

The raw denials from watchdog paint in interesting portrait:

```
type=1400 msg=audit(1417405598.000:8): avc: denied { create } for
pid=2267 comm="watchdogd" name="__null__" scontext=u:r:watchdogd:s0
tcontext=u:object_r:device:s0 tclass=chr_file

type=1400 msg=audit(1417405598.000:9): avc: denied { read write }
for pid=2267 comm="watchdogd" name="__null__" dev=tmpfs ino=2580
scontext=u:r:watchdogd:s0 tcontext=u:object_r:device:s0 tclass=chr_file

type=1400 msg=audit(1417405598.000:10): avc: denied { open } for
pid=2267 comm="watchdogd" name="__null__" dev=tmpfs ino=2580
scontext=u:r:watchdogd:s0 tcontext=u:object_r:device:s0 tclass=chr_file

type=1400 msg=audit(1417405598.000:11): avc: denied { unlink }
for pid=2267 comm="watchdogd" name="__null__" dev=tmpfs ino=2580
scontext=u:r:watchdogd:s0 tcontext=u:object_r:device:s0 tclass=chr_file
```

```
type=1400 msg=audit(1417416653.602:575): avc: denied { getattr } for
pid=3696 comm="onCtsTestRunner" path="/dev/watchdog" dev=tmpfs ino=1095
scontext=u:r:untrusted_app:s0:c512,c768 tcontext=u:object_r:watchdog_
device:s0 tclass=chr_file
```

A file is created and unlinked by `watchdog`, which keeps a handle to an anonymous file. No filesystem reference exists after the unlink, but the file descriptor is valid and only `watchdog` can use it. In this case, we can just allow watchdog this rule. In `watchdogd.te`, add `allow watchdogd device:chr_file create_file_perms;`. This rule, however, causes a `neverallow` violation in the base policy:

```
out/host/linux-x86/bin/checkpolicy: loading policy configuration from
out/target/product/udoo/obj/ETC/sepolicy_intermediates/policy.conf
libsepol.check_assertion_helper: neverallow on line 5375 violated by
allow watchdogd device:chr_file { read write open };
Error while expanding policy
```

The `neverallow` rule is in the `domain.te` base policy as `neverallow { domain -init -ueventd -recovery } device:chr_file { open read write };`. For such a simple change, we'll just modify the base sepolicy to `neverallow { domain -init -ueventd -recovery -watchdogd } device:chr_file { open read write };`.

wpa

```
#============= wpa ==============
allow wpa device:chr_file { read open };
allow wpa log_device:chr_file { write open };
allow wpa system_data_file:dir { write remove_name add_name setattr };
allow wpa system_data_file:sock_file { write create unlink setattr };
```

Again, the log device was handled in `domain.te`. The system data accesses need further investigation, starting with the raw denials:

```
type=1400 msg=audit(1417405614.060:193): avc: denied { setattr } for
pid=2639 comm="wpa_supplicant" name="wpa_supplicant" dev=mmcblk0p4
ino=129295 scontext=u:r:wpa:s0 tcontext=u:object_r:system_data_file:s0
tclass=dir
```

```
type=1400 msg=audit(1417405614.060:194): avc: denied { write } for
pid=2639 comm="wpa_supplicant" name="wlan0" dev=mmcblk0p4 ino=129318
scontext=u:r:wpa:s0 tcontext=u:object_r:system_data_file:s0 tclass=sock_
file
```

```
type=1400 msg=audit(1417405614.060:195): avc: denied { write } for
pid=2639 comm="wpa_supplicant" name="wpa_supplicant" dev=mmcblk0p4
ino=129295 scontext=u:r:wpa:s0 tcontext=u:object_r:system_data_file:s0
tclass=dir

type=1400 msg=audit(1417405614.060:196): avc: denied { remove_name } for
pid=2639 co
```

The offending file was located using `ls -laR`:

```
/data/system/wpa_supplicant:

srwxrwx--- wifi wifi 2014-12-01 06:43 wlan0
```

This socket is created by the `wpa_supplicant` itself. Relabeling it without type transitions is impossible, so we have to allow it. In `wpa.te`, add `allow wpa system_data_file:dir rw_dir_perms;` and `allow wpa system_data_file:sock_file create_file_perms;`. The unlabeled device has already been dealt with; it was on `rfkill`:

```
type=1400 msg=audit(1417405613.640:175): avc: denied { read } for
pid=2639 comm="wpa_supplicant" name="rfkill" dev=tmpfs ino=1126
scontext=u:r:wpa:s0 tcontext=u:object_r:device:s0 tclass=chr_file
```

Second policy pass

After loading the drafted policy, the device still has denials on boot:

```
#============= init ==============
allow init rootfs:file { write create };
allow init system_file:file execute_no_trans;
#============= shell ==============
allow shell device:chr_file { read write getattr };
allow shell system_file:file entrypoint;
```

All of these denials should be investigated because they target sensitive types, `tcontext` specifically.

init

The raw denials for `init` are as follows:

```
<5>type=1400 audit(4.380:3): avc: denied { create } for
pid=2268 comm="init" name="tasks" scontext=u:r:init:s0
tcontext=u:object_r:rootfs:s0 tclass=file

<5>type=1400 audit(4.380:4): avc: denied { write } for pid=2268
comm="init" name="tasks" dev=rootfs ino=3080 scontext=u:r:init:s0
tcontext=u:object_r:rootfs:s0 tclass=file
```

These occur before `init` remounts / as read-only. We can safely allow these, and since `init` is running unconfined, we can just add it to `init.te`. We could add the `allow` rule to the unconfined set, but since that is going away, let's minimize the permission only to `init`:

```
allow int rootfs:file create_file_perms;
```

 Unconfined is not completely unconfined. Rules get stripped from this domain as AOSP moves closer to zero unconfined domains.

Doing this, however, causes another `neverallow` to fail. We can modify `external/sepolicy domain.te` to bypass this. Change the `neverallow` from this:

```
# Nothing should be writing to files in the rootfs.
neverallow { domain -recovery} rootfs:file { create write setattr
relabelto append unlink link rename };
```

Change it to this:

```
# Nothing should be writing to files in the rootfs.
neverallow { domain -recovery -init } rootfs:file { create write
setattr relabelto append unlink link rename };
```

 If you need to modify `neverallow` entries to build, you will fail CTS. The proper approach is to remove this behavior from `init`.

Additionally, we need to see what is loaded with `exec` without a domain transition, causing the `execute_no_trans` denial:

```
<5>type=1400 audit(4.460:6): avc: denied { execute_no_trans } for
pid=2292 comm="init" path="/system/bin/magd" dev=mmcblk0p5 ino=146
scontext=u:r:init:s0 tcontext=u:object_r:system_file:s0 tclass=file

<5>type=1400 audit(4.460:6): avc: denied { execute_no_trans } for
pid=2292 comm="init" path="/system/bin/rfkill" dev=mmcblk0p5 ino=148
scontext=u:r:init:s0 tcontext=u:object_r:system_file:s0 tclass=file
```

To resolve this, we can relabel `magd` with its own type and place it in its own unconfined domain. A `neverallow` in the base policy forces us to move each executable into its own domain.

Create a file called `magd.te`, add it to `BOARD_SEPOLICY_UNION`, and add the following contents to it:

```
type magd, domain;
type magd_exec, exec_type, file_type;
permissive_or_unconfined(magd);
```

Also update `file_contexts` to contain this:

```
/system/bin/magd   u:object_r:magd_exec:s0
```

Repeat the steps that were done for `magd` for `rfkill`. Just replace `magd` with `rfkill` in the preceding example. Later testing revealed an entry-point denial where the source context was `init_shell` and the target was `rfkill_exec`. After adding the shell rules, it was discovered that `rfkill` is loaded using `exec` from the `init_ shell` domain, so let's also add `domain_auto_trans(init_shell, rfkill_exec, rfkill)` to the `rfkill.te` file. Additionally grouped with this discovery was `rfkill` attempting to open, read, and write `/dev/rfkill`. So we must label `/dev/ rfkill` with `rfkill_device`, allow `rfkill` access to it, and append `allow rfkill rfkill_device:chr_file rw_file_perms;` to the `rfkill.te` file. Create a new file to declare this device type, called `device.te`, and add `type rfkill_device, dev_type;`. After that, label it with `file_contexts` by adding `/dev/rfkill u:object_r:rfkill_device:s0`.

shell

The first shell denial we will evaluate is the denial on `entrypoint`:

```
<5>type=1400 audit(4.460:5): avc: denied { entrypoint } for
pid=2279 comm="init" path="/system/bin/mksh" dev=mmcblk0p5 ino=154
scontext=u:r:shell:s0 tcontext=u:object_r:system_file:s0 tclass=file
```

Since we did not label `mksh`, we need to label it now. We can create an unconfined domain for shells spawned by `init` to end up in the `init_shell` domain. The console still ends up in the `shell` domain via an explicit `seclabel`, and other invocations end up as `init_shell`. Create a new file, `init_shell.te`, and add it to `BOARD_SEPOLICY_UNION`.

init_shell.te

```
type init_shell, domain;
domain_auto_trans(init, shell_exec, init_shell);
permissive_or_unconfined(init_shell);
```

Update `file_contexts` to include this:

```
/system/bin/mksh   u:object_r:shell_exec:s0;
```

Now we will handle shell access to the raw device:

```
<5>type=1400 audit(6.510:7): avc: denied { read write } for pid=2279
comm="sh" name="ttymxc1" dev=tmpfs ino=122 scontext=u:r:shell:s0
tcontext=u:object_r:device:s0 tclass=chr_file

<5>type=1400 audit(7.339:8): avc: denied { getattr } for pid=2279
comm="sh" path="/dev/ttymxc1" dev=tmpfs ino=122 scontext=u:r:shell:s0
tcontext=u:object_r:device:s0 tclass=chr_file
```

This is just a mislabeled `tty`, so we can label this as a `tty_device`. Add the following entry to the file contexts:

```
/dev/ttymxc[0-9]*   u:object_r:tty_device:s0
```

Field trials

At this point, rebuild the source tree, wipe the data filesystem, flash, and re-run CTS. Repeat this until all denials are addressed.

Once you're done with CTS and internal QA trials, we recommend performing a field trial with the device in permissive mode. During this period, you should be gathering the logs and refining policy. If the domains are not stable, you can declare them as permissive in the policy file and still put the device in enforcing mode; enforcing some domains is better than enforcing none.

Going enforcing

You can pass the enforcing mode either using `bootloader` (which will not be covered here) or with the `init.rc` script early in boot time. You can do this right after `setcon`:

```
setcon u:r:init:s0
setenforce 1
```

Once this statement is compiled into the `init.rc` script, it can only be undone with a subsequent build and a reflash of `boot.img`. You can check this by running the `getenforce` command. Also, as an interesting test, you can try to run the `reboot` command from the root serial console and watch it fail:

```
root@udoo:/ # getenforce

Enforcing

root@udoo:/ # reboot

reboot: Operation not permitted
```

Summary

In this chapter, all of your previous understanding of the system was used to develop real SE for Android policy for a brand new device. You are now empowered with the knowledge of how to write SELinux policy for Android, where and how the components of the system work, and how to port and enable these features on various Android platforms. Since this is a fairly new feature that influences many system interactions, issues that will require code changes as well as policy changes will arise. Understanding both is crucial.

As policy authors and security personnel in general, the responsibility to secure the system rests on our shoulders. In most organizations, you're required to work in the dark. However, if you can, do as much work and ask as many questions as you want to in the mailing list, and never accept the status quo. The SE for Android and AOSP projects welcome all to contribute, and by contributing, you will help make the project better and enhance the feature sets for all.

The Development Environment

In order to build the Android 4.3 sources provided by UDOO, you need an Ubuntu Linux system with Oracle Java 6. While it may be possible to use a variant of this setup, Google's standard target development platform for Android 4.3 is Ubuntu 12.04. Therefore, we will use this setup to ensure the highest probability of success in our exploration of Linux, SE Linux, Android, the UDOO, and SE for Android.

In this appendix, we will do the following:

- Download and install Ubuntu 12.04 using a **virtual machine (VM)**
- Enhance our VM's performance by installing the VirtualBox Extension Pack and VirtualBox Guest Additions
- Set up a development environment appropriate for building the Linux kernel and UDOO sources
- Install Oracle Java 6

If you already use Ubuntu Linux 12.04, you can skip to the *The Build Environment* section. If you intend to install Ubuntu natively (not in a VM), you should skip to the *Ubuntu Linux 12.04* section and follow those directions, ignoring the VirtualBox steps.

VirtualBox

There are a number of virtualization products available for running guest operating systems, such as Ubuntu Linux, but for this setup we will use **VirtualBox**. VirtualBox is a widely used open source virtualization system available for Mac, Linux, Solaris, and Windows hosts (among others). It supports a variety of guest operating systems. VirtualBox also allows the use of hardware virtualization of many modern/common processor families to increase performance by providing each virtual machine its own private address space.

The VirtualBox documentation has excellent installation instructions for various platforms, and we recommend referring to these for your host platform. You can find information about installing and running VirtualBox for your host operating system at `http://www.virtualbox.org/manual/ch02.html`.

Ubuntu Linux 12.04 (precise pangolin)

To install Ubuntu Linux 12.04, you will first need to download an appropriate distribution image. These can be found at `http://releases.ubuntu.com/12.04/`. While there are a number of acceptable images there, we will install the 64-bit desktop version of the distribution—`http://releases.ubuntu.com/12.04/ubuntu-12.04.5-desktop-amd64.iso`. The host machine we're using in this example is a 64-bit Macbook Pro running OS X 10.9.2, so we're targeting a 64-bit guest as well. If you have a 32-bit machine, the basic mechanics of what we cover will be the same; only a few details will be different, so we will leave those for you to discover and resolve.

Launch VirtualBox on your host, wait for the **VM Manager** window to appear, and perform the following steps:

1. Click on **New**.
2. For the **Name** and **Operating System** settings, make the following selections:
   - **Name: SE for Android Book**
   - **Type: Linux**
   - **Version: Ubuntu (64 bit)**
3. Set **Memory Size** to a value to at least 16 GB. Anything lower than this will lead to unsuccessful builds.
4. To set up the hard drive, select **Create a virtual hard drive now**. Set this value to at least 80 GB.

5. Choose the **Hard Drive File Type**, **VDI (VirtualBox Disk Image)**.

6. Ensure storage on the physical hard drive is set to **dynamically allocated**.

7. When prompted for **file location and size**, name the new virtual hard drive **SE for Android Book**, and set its size to 80 GB.

Ensure the **SE for Android Book** VM is selected in the left pane. Click on the green Start arrow to perform an initial launch of the VM. A dialog will appear, asking you to select a virtual optical disk file. Click on the small folder icon and locate the `ubuntu-12.04.5-desktop-amd64.iso` CD image you downloaded earlier. Then click on **Start**.

When the screen turns black and shows a keyboard image at the bottom center of the VM window, press any key to begin the Ubuntu installation. As soon as you do this, the language selection screen will appear. Choose whichever language is most appropriate for you, but for this example, we'll select **English**. Then select **Install Ubuntu**.

Sometimes, you may see an unusual-looking error printed across your VM window—something like **SMBus base address uninitialized**. This message is shown because VirtualBox doesn't support a particular kernel module that is loaded by default with Ubuntu 12.04. However, this will not cause any difficulty and is only a cosmetic annoyance. After a few moments, a nice GUI installation screen will appear, waiting for you to choose a language again. We'll choose **English** again.

On the following **Preparing to install Ubuntu** screen, three checklist items are shown. You should have already satisfied the first item, since your virtual drive is much larger than the minimum requirement for Ubuntu. To satisfy the others, ensure your host system is plugged in with a power supply and has an established network connection. Although this is entirely unnecessary for our purposes here, we almost always mark the **Download updates while installing** and **Install this third-party software** boxes before continuing.

On the **Installation type** screen, we'll take the easy path and select **Erase disk and install Ubuntu**. Keep in mind that this will only erase the disk of your VM's virtual hard drive and leaves your host system intact. On the **Erase disk and install Ubuntu** screen, your virtual hard drive should already be selected, so you only need to click **Install Now**.

From this point forward in the Ubuntu installation, two separate tasks will happen simultaneously: in a background thread, the installer will prepare the virtual drive for the installation of the base system; secondly, you will configure some basic aspects of your new system. But first, you will have to identify your time zone by clicking on the appropriate point on the world map before continuing. Then identify your keyboard layout and continue.

Set up your first user account. In this case, it will be the account we used to do the work in this book, so we will enter the following information:

- **Your Name**: Book User
- **Your computer's name**: SE-for-Android
- **Pick a username**: bookuser
- **Password fields**: (whatever you prefer)

We will also select **Log in automatically**. While we would not normally do this for security reasons, we will do it in our local VM for convenience; but you may protect this account in whichever way you prefer.

Once the Ubuntu installation is complete, a dialog asking you to restart the computer will appear. Click the **Restart now** button, and after a few moments, a terminal prompt will inform you to remove all installation media and press *Enter*. To remove the virtual installation CD, go to **Devices | CD/DVD Devices | Remove disk from virtual drive** using the VirtualBox menu bar. Then press *Enter* to restart the VM, but interrupt the boot process by closing the VM window. It will ask you if you want to power off the machine. Just click **OK**.

VirtualBox extension pack and guest additions

To get the best performance from your guest Ubuntu VM and access to the virtual USB devices necessary for working with the UDOO, you will need to install the VirtualBox extension pack and guest additions.

VirtualBox extension pack

Download the extension pack from the VirtualBox website, at `http://www.virtualbox.org/wiki/Downloads`. There will be a download link there intended for **All supported platforms**. Once this file is downloaded, you'll need to install it. This process is different for each type of host system, but it is very straightforward. For Linux and Mac OS X hosts, simply double-clicking on the downloaded extension pack file will do the trick. For Windows systems, you will need to run the installer you've downloaded.

VirtualBox guest additions

Once you've completed the installation of the extension pack, boot your Ubuntu Linux 12.04 VM from VirtualBox by selecting the VM from the left pane and clicking on **Start** in the toolbar. Once your Ubuntu desktop is active, you'll notice it does not fit into your VM window. Resize the VM window to make it larger, and the VM screen will remain the same size. This, among other performance issues, will be resolved by installing the VirtualBox guest additions. You may also see a window open on your virtual desktop indicating a new version of Ubuntu is available. Do not upgrade; just close that window.

Using the VirtualBox menu bar, go to **Devices | Insert Guest Additions CD Image....** Shortly afterward, a dialog will appear, asking whether you want to run the software on the new media you just inserted. Click the **Run** button. You will then need to authenticate your user by entering your user's password (which you entered during setup). Once the user is authenticated, a script will automatically build and update several kernel modules. Once the script completes, reboot the VM by clicking on the gear in the top-right corner of the screen, selecting **Shutdown...**, and clicking on **Restart** in the dialog that follows.

When the VM reboots, the first thing you should notice is that the VM screen now fits into the VM window. Moreover, if you resize the VM window, the VM screen resizes with it. This is the simplest way to determine you've successfully installed the VirtualBox guest additions.

Save time with shared folders

Another thing you can do to boost your aggregate performance while developing images for the UDOO is to set up shared folders between your host system and your Ubuntu Linux guest system. In this way, once you've built a new SD card image for the UDOO, you can make the image directly available to the host through the shared folder. The host can then execute the long-running commands to flash the SD card without adding time to the process by slowing down access to your host's card reader through the virtualization layer. In the case of the system we're using to write this book, there is a savings of around 10 minutes per image flashed.

To set up a shared folder, you must begin with the VirtualBox Manager open and your Ubuntu VM powered off. Click the **Settings** toolbar icon. Then select the **Shared Folders** tab of the **Settings** dialog that opens. Click the **Add Shared Folder** icon to the right. Enter **Folder Path** to a folder on your host that you want to share. In our case, we created a new folder called `vbox_share` to share with our VM guest. VirtualBox will generate **Folder Name**, but make sure you select **Auto-mount** before clicking **OK**. When you boot your Ubuntu VM from now on, the shared folder will be accessible in your guest VM as `/media/sf_<folder_name>`. However, if you attempt to list the files in that directory from your guest, you will likely be denied. To gain full access to this folder (as in read-and-write access) for our `bookuser`, we'll need to add that UID to the `vboxsf` group:

```
$ sudo usermod -a -G vboxsf bookuser
```

Log out and log in to your guest again or restart the guest VM to complete the process.

The build environment

To prepare our system to build the Linux kernel, Android, and Android applications, we need to install and set up some key pieces of software. Click the Ubuntu dashboard icon at the top of the launch bar on the left of your screen. In the search bar that appears, type `term` and press *Enter*. A terminal window will open. Then execute the following commands:

```
$ sudo apt-get update
```

```
$ sudo apt-get install apt-file git-core gnupg flex bison gperf build-
essential zip curl zlib1g-dev libc6-dev lib32ncurses5-dev ia32-libs
x11proto-core-dev libx11-dev ia32-libs dialog liblzo2-dev libxml2-utils
minicom
```

Type `y` and press *Enter* when asked whether you want to continue.

Oracle Java 6

Download the most recent Java 6 SE Development Kit (version 6u45) from the Oracle Java archive website, at `http://www.oracle.com/technetwork/java/javase/archive-139210.html`. You'll need the `jdk-6u45-linux-x64.bin` version to satisfy Google's target development environment. Once it is downloaded, execute the following commands to install the Java 6 JDK:

```
$ chmod a+x jdk-6u45-linux-x64.bin
```

```
$ sudo mkdir -p /usr/lib/jvm
```

```
$ sudo mv jdk-6u45-linux-x64.bin /usr/lib/jvm/

$ cd /usr/lib/jvm/

$ sudo ./jdk-6u45-linux-x64.bin

$ sudo update-alternatives --install "/usr/bin/java" "java" "/usr/lib/
jvm/jdk1.6.0_45/bin/java" 1

$ sudo update-alternatives --install "/usr/bin/jar" "jar" "/usr/lib/jvm/
jdk1.6.0_45/bin/jar" 1

$ sudo update-alternatives --install "/usr/bin/javac" "javac" "/usr/lib/
jvm/jdk1.6.0_45/bin/javac" 1

$ sudo update-alternatives --install "/usr/bin/javaws" "javaws" "/usr/
lib/jvm/jdk1.6.0_45/bin/javaws" 1

$ sudo update-alternatives --install "/usr/bin/jar" "jar" "/usr/lib/jvm/
jdk1.6.0_35/bin/jar" 1

$ sudo update-alternatives --install "/usr/bin/javadoc" "javadoc" "/usr/
lib/jvm/jdk1.6.0_45/bin/javadoc" 1

$ sudo update-alternatives --install "/usr/bin/jarsigner" "jarsigner" "/
usr/lib/jvm/jdk1.6.0_45/bin/jarsigner" 1

$ sudo update-alternatives --install "/usr/bin/javah" "javah" "/usr/lib/
jvm/jdk1.6.0_45/bin/javah" 1

$ sudo rm jdk-6u45-linux-x64.bin
```

Summary

In this appendix, we discussed Google's target development environment for
Android and showed how to create a compatible environment, potentially in a
virtual machine. You should feel free to modify other elements of your system, but
having the elements of this appendix installed will provide you with the minimally
viable environment necessary to perform all the steps outlined in *Chapter 4,
Installation on the UDOO,* and beyond.

Index

A

Access Vector Cache 68, 69
access vectors
  about 24
  call 36
  impersonate 36
  set_context_mgr 36
  transfer 36
Activity Manager Service (AMS) 36
Android
  about 7
  DAC, using for 17
  security model 31-33
Android Debug Bridge (adb) 46-49
Android Interface Description
       Language (AIDL) 35
Android.mk, sepolicy
  build_policy, defining 155, 156
  exploring 149
  file_contexts, building 158
  mac_permissions.xml, building 157
  NSA research files 158
  policy build, controlling 152-155
  property_contexts, building 158
  seapp_contexts, building 158
  sepolicy, building 150, 151
Android Open Source Community
       (AOSP) 75
Android versions
  URL 38
Android vulnerabilities
  about 17
  CVE-2010-EASY 18
  GingerBreak 18

  MotoChopper 19
  Skype vulnerability 18
AOSP devices
  URL 76
APK 119
app labeling
  limitations 118
applications 32
auditd daemon 80
auditd internals 81, 82
audit logs 165
audit system
  about 79
  auditd daemon 80
  auditd internals 81, 82

B

Binder
  about 33
  and security 36
  architecture 34, 35
  features 34
binder patch
  URL 76
booleans directory 69, 70
build environment 188
build_policy
  defining 155, 156

C

cache_threshold file 69
capabilities model 16, 17
chcon command 101
class directory 70, 71

Compatibility Definition Document
     (CDD) **163**
Compatibility Test Suite (CTS)
  about 70, 87
  URL 70
contexts
  about 85, 86
  domains, mapping 86, 87
control properties 144
CTS
  running 163, 164
  setting up 163
  URL 114
CTS binary
  URL 163
CTS results
  audit logs 165
  CTS test results 164
  gathering 164

D

DAC
  about 7
  used, for Android 17
define keyword 112
device
  purging 162
device policy
  adbd 165-168
  authoring 165
  bootanim 169
  debuggerd 170
  drmserver 170
  dumpstate 171
  installd 171
  keystore 172
  mediaserver 172
  netd 173
  rild 173
  servicemanager 173
  surfaceflinger 173
  system_server 174
  toolbox 174
  untrusted_app 175, 176
  vold 176

watchdogd 176, 177
wpa 177, 178
disable file interface 66
Discretionary Access Controls. *See* **DAC**
dynamic domain transitions 111-113
dynamic type transitions 95
dyntransition 72

E

enforce file 65
enforcing mode
  passing 181
existing properties
  relabeling 141-143
explicit contexts
  via seclabel 113
extended attributes
  labeling with 92

F

field trials 181
file_contexts file
  about 93, 94
  building 158
filesystem
  Access Vector Cache 68, 69
  booleans directory 69, 70
  class directory 70, 71
  disable file interface 66
  dynamic type transitions 95
  enforce file 65
  extended attributes 92
  file_contexts file 93, 94
  fs_task_use 90
  fs_use 90
  fs_use_trans 91
  genfscon 91
  initial_contexts directory 71
  interrogating 64
  labeling 89
  locating 63, 64
  mls file 67
  mount options 92

null file 67
policy_capabilities directory 72
policy file 66
procfs 72, 73
status file 67
FLASK 22
fs_task_use file 90
fs_use file 90
fs_use_trans file 91

G

getenforce command, states
  disabled 62
  enforcing 62
  permissive 62
GingerBreak 18
graphical menu
  settings 42
groups
  changing 14

I

initial_contexts directory 71
init process 105-111
Interprocess Communication (IPC) 33

J

Java SELinux API 73

K

kernel
  SELinux, enabling in 53
kernel-common project
  URL 76
keys.conf file 129

L

labeling
  via property_contexts 139
labels
  about 23
  roles 23

types 23, 24
users 23
Linux Security Module (LSM) 22, 36

M

mac_permissions.xml file
  about 126-129
  building 157
mls file 67
MotoChopper 19
mount options 92
multilevel security (MLS) 24, 67

N

National Security Agency (NSA) 36
NSA repositories
  URL 76
NSA research files 158
null file 67

O

Oracle Java 6 188
Oracle Java archive
  URL 188
owners
  changing 14

P

patches 76-79
permission bits
  changing 10-14
permissions, on properties 140
permissive 65
persistent properties 144
pet analogy
  about 25-29
  URL 25
policy build
  controlling 152-155
policy_capabilities directory 72
policy file 66
policy load 56-59

policy pass
  about 178
  init 178, 179
  init_shell.te 181
  shell 180
policy version
  fixing 60-62
processes
  about 8
  relabeling 114-117
Process ID (PID) 34, 105
procfs 72, 73
projects
  building 147-149
properties
  creating 143, 144
  labeling 143, 144
property_contexts file
  building 158
  labeling via 139
property service 38

R

Radio Interface Layer Daemon
    (RILD) 32, 106
README
  media 120
  platform 120
  shared 120
  testkey 120
Red Hat Enterprise Linux (RHEL) 22
role-based access controls (RBAC) 23
roles, labels 23

S

seapp_contexts file
  about 130-137
  building 158
security
  and Binder 36
Security Enhanced Linux. See SELinux
security model
  applications 32
  system component services 32

SELinux
  about 22
  benefits 25
  best practices 30
  complexities 30
  enabling, in kernel 53
  implementing 24
  properties 145
  denial logs, interpreting 83-85
sepolicy
  building 150, 151
sepolicy-analyze tool 159, 160
sepolicy-check tool 159
SEPolicy master
  updating 161, 162
shared folders 187
Skype vulnerability 18
source
  retrieving 42-44
special properties
  about 144
  control properties 144
  persistent properties 144
  SELinux properties 145
standalone tools
  about 159
  sepolicy-analyze 159, 160
  sepolicy-check 159
status file 67
supplementary groups 8
switch
  flipping 49-52
system
  apps 119
  component services 32
  server 33

T

targets
  about 22
  building 147-149
tools, filesystems
  /data filesystem, fixing up 103
  about 96-102
  security 104

type enforcement (TE) 23, 112
type field value, filesystem object
  -- 93
  -b 93
  -c 93
  -d 93
  -l 93
  -p 93
  -s 93
  about 93
types, labels 23, 24

U

Ubuntu Linux 12.04
  about 184-186
  URL 184
UDOO Android 4.3 Jelly Bean source code
  URL 41
UDOO documentation
  URL 42
UDOO serial 46-48
user-based access controls (UBAC) 23
users, labels 23
userspace object manager 67

V

variables
  BOARD_SEPOLICY_DIRS 152
  BOARD_SEPOLICY_IGNORE 152
  BOARD_SEPOLICY_REPLACE 152
  BOARD_SEPOLICY_UNION 152
VirtualBox
  about 184
  extension pack 186
  guest additions 187
  URL 184
virtual machine (VM) 37, 183

Z

zygote
  fortifying 120, 121
  keys.conf 129
  mac_permissions.xml file 126-129
  seapp_contexts 130-137
  securing 119, 120
  zygote socket, plumbing 121-126

Thank you for buying
Exploring SE for Android

About Packt Publishing

Packt, pronounced 'packed', published its first book, *Mastering phpMyAdmin for Effective MySQL Management*, in April 2004, and subsequently continued to specialize in publishing highly focused books on specific technologies and solutions.

Our books and publications share the experiences of your fellow IT professionals in adapting and customizing today's systems, applications, and frameworks. Our solution-based books give you the knowledge and power to customize the software and technologies you're using to get the job done. Packt books are more specific and less general than the IT books you have seen in the past. Our unique business model allows us to bring you more focused information, giving you more of what you need to know, and less of what you don't.

Packt is a modern yet unique publishing company that focuses on producing quality, cutting-edge books for communities of developers, administrators, and newbies alike. For more information, please visit our website at www.packtpub.com.

About Packt Open Source

In 2010, Packt launched two new brands, Packt Open Source and Packt Enterprise, in order to continue its focus on specialization. This book is part of the Packt Open Source brand, home to books published on software built around open source licenses, and offering information to anybody from advanced developers to budding web designers. The Open Source brand also runs Packt's Open Source Royalty Scheme, by which Packt gives a royalty to each open source project about whose software a book is sold.

Writing for Packt

We welcome all inquiries from people who are interested in authoring. Book proposals should be sent to author@packtpub.com. If your book idea is still at an early stage and you would like to discuss it first before writing a formal book proposal, then please contact us; one of our commissioning editors will get in touch with you.

We're not just looking for published authors; if you have strong technical skills but no writing experience, our experienced editors can help you develop a writing career, or simply get some additional reward for your expertise.

Android Security Cookbook

ISBN: 978-1-78216-716-7   Paperback: 350 pages

Practical recipes to delve into Android's security mechanisms by troubleshooting common vulnerabilities in applications and Android OS versions

1. Analyze the security of Android applications and devices, and exploit common vulnerabilities in applications and Android operating systems.

2. Develop custom vulnerability assessment tools using the Drozer Android Security Assessment Framework.

3. Reverse-engineer Android applications for security vulnerabilities.

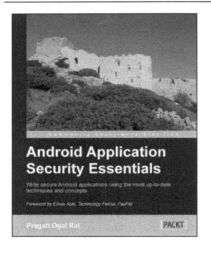

Android Application Security Essentials

ISBN: 978-1-84951-560-3   Paperback: 218 pages

Write secure Android applications using the most up-to-date techniques and concepts

1. Understand Android security from kernel to the application layer.

2. Protect components using permissions.

3. Safeguard user and corporate data from prying eyes.

4. Understand the security implications of mobile payments, NFC, and more.

Please check **www.PacktPub.com** for information on our titles

Testing and Securing Android Studio Applications

ISBN: 978-1-78398-880-8   Paperback: 162 pages

Debug and secure your Android applications with Android Studio

1. Explore the foundations of security and learn how to apply these measures to create secure applications using Android Studio.

2. Create effective test cases, unit tests, and functional tests to ensure your Android applications function correctly.

3. Optimize the performance of your app by debugging and using high-quality code.

Android Native Development Kit Cookbook

ISBN: 978-1-84969-150-5   Paperback: 346 pages

A step-by-step tutorial with more than 60 concise recipes on Android NDK development skills

1. Build, debug, and profile Android NDK apps.

2. Implement part of Android apps in native C/C++ code.

3. Optimize code performance in assembly with Android NDK.

Please check **www.PacktPub.com** for information on our titles